CW01085423

THE ART OF DECONDITIONING

REFERENCE MATERIAL

LIBRARY | SERVICES

CAMDEN | 1974

THE STANDARD, LONDON

Reading is Fundamental

REFERENCE LIBRARY

THE STANDARD LONDON
Reading is
Fundamental
REFERENCE LIBRARY

THE ART OF DECONDITIONING

Who says freedom is distant

Ajay Kapoor

For any help about reaching the state of freedom,

Email: ajay@zmeditation.com

Website: www.zmeditation.com

Phones: 91-9313649756, 9318678903, 9418036956

Address: Z Meditation Center, Village Kandi, PO

Khanyara, Dharamsala, India 176218

Everybody can freely use the contents of this book for reference.

Dedication

The life of the author(?)
is dedicated to his Source.

Table of Contents

Introduction

1. This book is not an invention. It is just a recap of The Eternal Principles that govern human mind. It states in a concise manner how to be happily fulfilled.

2. These Eternal Principles revealed themselves again in the meditations of the author who was just a seer.

3. When you will understand and practice them, you will start appreciating and accepting the following way of living:

   a. Unconditioned Peace, i.e., detachment from desires and expectations.

   b. Freedom from all wrong notions and conditionings.

   c. Living in total harmony with the Truth.

   d. Unconditioned love for one and all.

4. It has been received and presented in a manner that is clearly suited to those who want to first understand and then practice. If there is disagreement on any point, ask questions and proceed further only when you are satisfied. Make use of email to contact the author.

5. This work has been named Z Meditation – 'Z' denotes the highest possibility for a human being.

6. 'Meditation' means detachment from the mind and realizing a state of unconditioned peace, love and freedom. Meditation is the means as well as the end.

Purpose of Meditation

Coming Home

The sweetest and highest possibility for a human being is to live in unconditioned happiness and love. But when you look around, you see that almost everybody is living far away from this pristine state of being. The vision of Z Meditation is to bring those who are sincere and willing back home. Those who have gone away from themselves, but want to come back to their inner center, may need some compassionate help, guidance and tools to be able to do so. Z Meditation is serving this cause since 1997.

Coming home is possible by gaining and practicing right knowledge. It also requires letting go of the wrong knowledge. If you see a snake in a rope, you get scared. In reality, you are getting scared because of your wrong vision. The snake is not there. You are only imagining that it is there. In order to get rid of your fear, it is necessary that you give up your illusion and acquire right understanding. As soon as the imaginary snake disappears, you will be peaceful.

11

You don't need to do anything else. Yes, you don't need to do anything else. Just do deep contemplation and get rid of the wrong notions. Gain right knowledge. And practice sincerely. You shall obtain freedom from all fears and insecurities. You will naturally become peaceful and happy. There is no need to do any difficult postures! There is no need to do any esoteric mantras; there is no need to do even those difficult visualizations. All these exercises that are taught in the name of meditation are just the initial preparatory warm-ups to gain stability. They are helpful for the beginners. But they don't change the understanding of the practitioner. The transformation of the understanding is a different game altogether. *Transformation and Upliftment of the Perspective is The Way. Letting go of the illusions is The Path.*

The purpose of meditation is to elevate the mind to its highest possibility of unconditioned peace and love. There are various rungs that a meditator must climb in this process. It begins with **studying or listening** to the right knowledge. The test of rightness is that it should be experientiable by each and everybody. If it is not and if things appear to be mysterious, there could be something wrong or very ordinary. **The highest knowledge is always the simplest one. There is nothing esoteric about it.**

Having listened to, one needs to **deeply contemplate** upon the truth. When one does that, it gets **integrated** with one's life in due course. The speed of progress depends upon the sincerity of the seeker. If spiritual growth becomes one's topmost priority in life, the destination can be reached very rapidly. We have seen people experiencing the higher states of consciousness within a few days of the work.

These are the various rungs of meditation practice:

1. Freedom from wrong notions, conditionings and the resultant suffering: Deep DeConditioning Inquiry will be employed for this purpose. This is the first level of practice. This book will teach the theory of meditation and six questions of Deep DeConditioning Inquiry.

2. Establishment in right understanding, unconditioned happiness and unconditioned love: Six Radiant Mantras will be learned and practiced in the second part of the book. These Mantras help us fully live in the moment.

3. Experiencing the Eternal Blissful Awareness as one's true identity: as the Inquiry deepens further in the third level, one reaches this sublime state of eternal freedom.

4. Merging in the Absolute: All props drop in the end.

And things happen in this order only. Unless you free yourself from your illusions, you cannot be peaceful. If you are not peaceful, your happiness cannot be stable. If you are not happy, your mind will keep running after the objects that you believe will give you happiness. With this restless mind, you cannot meditate and experience **Eternal Blissful Awareness** as your true identity. The question of merging in the absolute does not arise if you don't know your true identity.

In this book, you will first gain the understanding of the functioning of your mind. The philosophy and practice of meditation will be taught in a progressive way so that even the beginners can grasp this subtle knowledge.

This book is about the first level of learning: Deep Deconditioning Inquiry. The other three levels can be learnt and practiced at the silent retreats of Z Meditation.

Five principles of meditation

No proof, No Belief

All beliefs should be scientifically validated. Everybody should be able to experience the beliefs if they are true. That is, the beliefs become science when they are objective.

No Concepts, No Peace

There is zero possibility of *suppressing* the turbulence of the mind by mechanical means. For lasting peace, the concepts must be understood clearly.

No Mother-tongue, No Understanding

One thinks best in one's own language. Without deep thinking, one cannot integrate the knowledge with one's real life. Using a language that one does not understand makes things mysterious and difficult to grasp.

No Tuning, No Music

Meditation does not mean torturing the body or the mind. It is an enjoyable and radiant way to clear the mind of turmoil. It makes one see things in the Light of Truth. The middle path is the best path, i.e., moderation in eating, sleeping and recreation is helpful for meditation. If one is into self affliction and torture, one cannot think clearly. Without clear thinking, one cannot detach from one's age-old conditionings.

No Integration, No Dance

Meditation is a way of life and not just a routine. If the rest of the day is not lived in conformity with what one practices in one's meditation, one cannot make progress just by doing some monotonous and mechanical exercises.

These are revolutionary principles of meditation. Integrating them with one's practice, one can make speedy and enduring progress in this beautiful mind-elevation game.

Objectives of the book

1. To recognize and remove all the illusions of understanding.

2. To experientially understand the difference between dreaming and living in reality.

3. To develop a skill for removing the mental clutter.

4. To develop an expertise of filtering the feelings from this clutter.

5. To understand the functioning of the mind – your own as well as that of people around you – and gain awareness about the *Causal Platforms* from where people operate. Once you have the knowledge about these platforms, you learn to remain balanced even in the most difficult inter-personal situations.

6. To understand and appreciate why people are not peaceful and learn to apply the Laws of Peace in one's own life.

7. To understand and experience the real meaning of Freedom which is nothing but detachment from all wrong conditionings.

8. To understand the damaging effects of interfering in others' business and to be trained in living in one's own real business.

9. To know what it means and takes to live in the Here and Now.

Those who have deconditioned themselves will be very well equipped to face any challenge in life. They will have learnt to use a tool that can be employed in every situation in order to remove the mental clutter and live in a state of pure joy and compassion.

Some useful hints

1. It is a book for learning how to do profound contemplation for spiritual growth. You will learn how to detach yourself from your mental turmoil and do Deep Inquiry. The Inquiry will elevate your mind to the state of freedom in no time.

2. Each chapter is written in the form of meditative points. Study one point. Stop and contemplate. Integrate it with your mindset. Digest it well and then move forward.

3. When you go to your place of work, apply the concepts there. Meditation ought not to finish on the meditation seat. It is a way of life.

4. In the evening, do the revision. Sit down again to contemplate. See for yourself if you lived up to the principles or not. Ask yourself: 'What more can I do?'

5. There are many short true stories used in the course. These stories are meant to understand the process of deep inquiry. They will culminate toward the end. The names have been changed in these stories.

6. If you find terseness anywhere, it is a deliberate attempt to make you contemplate. Try to bridge the gaps on your own. If you have doubts or need clarifications, please send email to the author.

Thinking v/s Dreaming

In order to have good concentration,
snap yourself out of daydreams.

1. In order to see for yourself the current state of your mind, do a simple concentration exercise. Keep a pen and notebook with you. Sit straight and focus on your breath. When you inhale, in your mind, say 'Om'; and on exhaling, do reverse counting from one hundred. One count with each breath. If, on the way down, some thoughts disturb you, note them down and start all over again. Do this for half an hour.

2. After half an hour, study yourself in your notebook. You might have written tens of thoughts. You might also have forgotten so many others. You will see that most of the thoughts are incoherent and futile. You will also appreciate that most of the time, you remained *lost* in these thoughts and you could not have a smooth flow of concentration.

3. The 'Om' and counting thoughts are your intentional and voluntary thoughts. They represent *thinking*. You can call them **thinking thoughts**.

4. All the other thoughts are *coming* to you involuntarily and unconsciously. Most of the time, you remain drowned in this ocean of thoughtlessness. These involuntary thoughts are random, uncontrolled and disjointed. You may call them **dream thoughts** – as they make all our day dreams.

5. There are certain properties of a restless mind that remains lost in the dream thoughts:

a. Dreaming most the time, i.e., extreme restlessness.

b. Desire to change the future or past.

c. Worrying or regretting about the future or past.

d. Inability to live and enjoy the present moment.

e. Running in circles, especially when facing a problem.

f. Lack of awareness.

6. **It is *either* the thinking *or* the dream thoughts that can occupy the mind *at a time*.** You cannot dream and have voluntary thoughts also at the same time.

7. **The current state of restlessness is not accidental.** You are consciously or unconsciously choosing what to have in your minds and what not to. You don't get the President of Libya in your dreams – there is a reason for that. You get

your relatives and friends in your dreams – there is a reason for that too.

8. **Thinking or dreaming – make a choice.** We can become the masters of our minds by learning to choose which type of thoughts to have and which not.

Illusion of Duality

You just experience yourself all the time.

John Mayor, a resident of San Francisco, had to go to New York for some office work. His wife, Nancy, wanted to accompany him as she was a little suspicious about his behavior since the past few days. He had been regularly coming back late. John was not happy with the idea of Nancy going to New York with him. He hated all the unnecessary fuss that her senseless suspicion was creating. They had a big fight over this issue and John left the house in disgust. He was now planning to go for divorce.

1. The whole episode lasted for fifteen minutes only. Thank God, it was just a bad dream! John got up and saw the time. 3 am. He smiled and looked at Nancy who was snoring very gently. He decided to go to his meditation room and reflect on the dream.

2. John understood that it was just his mind's play. It was his own mind that had assumed various names and forms in the dream. There was nothing that had happened in reality. He himself had become San Francisco, New York, Nancy, commotion, thoughts about divorce etc. He himself had also

become all the feelings like disgust and anger. Everything was his mind's creation. In the dream state, the subject of the dream, John Mayor, and all the objects experienced, were coming from the same source – him. He was experiencing just his mental formations.

3. When he woke up, i.e., in the waking state, the knower of the dream was also he himself.

4. As John was contemplating, he asked himself some questions: Just like the dreams at night, am I not lost in daydreams during the day too? What is it that I experience when I am daydreaming? Is it not that I am becoming my dreams and when I am lost in them, I mistakenly consider them to be reality? Was my suffering in that night dream justified? What is it that I suffered about? Is my suffering during daytime justified? What is it that I suffer about?

5. When you are lost in the dream state, you wrongly believe that you are experiencing many distinct objects or people having their separate identities. You experience only yourself – your mind. You just have the illusion of duality. The objects of your dream have no identity apart from you – as the waves have no separate identity apart from water.

Illusion of Reality

While you dream, you are invariably lost.
You wrongly take it to be reality.

1. Think about this question for a while: 'In the dream state, when John was arguing with his wife, could he do anything different?'

2. Actually, this question is an absurd question as we cannot ever know that we are dreaming while the dream is going on. **It is only on waking up that our reality perception changes** and we come to a position of understanding and analyzing.

3. In the waking state of consciousness, when we are apparently awake but actually dreaming, what is it that we experience? Is it not our own mental formations here also?

4. On waking up, John understood that while the dream was going on, he was unaware that it was a dream. **During that period of dreaming, he was wrongly considering the experience to be real.** That is why, he was feeling unhappy and stressed. **This is the illusion of reality.**

5. The substance of at least ninety-five percent of our experiences is our own imaginations because we spend all this time of our lives in dreaming! We are so lost in them that there hardly occurs a moment in the lives of most of us when we come out and are objective about them.

6. All our suffering is happening in dreams only! **When there is awareness, there cannot be suffering**. When John is awake, is he still suffering because Nancy was suspicious in the dream?

7. **When dream thoughts are there, one's awareness sleeps and when awareness awakens, dreaming disappears.**

8. In order to have awareness, which is a necessary pre-requisite for meditation, we need to learn to snap ourselves out of our dreams.

Illusion of Incompleteness

'I + X = C' is an illusion

1. All of us wish to achieve a state of completeness and fulfillment. Nobody here wants to be incomplete or dissatisfied. It is only when this state of inner wholeness is experienced that one can be truly happy.

2. However, the experience of most people is just the opposite. Despite an ingrained desire to be complete and therefore happy, we feel a sense of lacking?

3. Is this a real incompleteness or imaginary – please think?

4. Contemplate and write down your definitions of reality and imagination.

5. This incompleteness is imaginary. There are two imaginary equations of incompleteness that we believe in:
   $I + X = Completeness$
   $I – X = Incompleteness$
   The X in these equations can be money, people, situation, environment, job, place, time etc. We believe that there is something incomplete in us and we will remove it with the fulfillment of our desires related to our X factors.

6. If these equations were true, how would these facts be explained:

a. The same X giving happiness now and unhappiness at another time i.e., happiness diminishing with time.

b. The same X giving happiness to one and unhappiness to another at the same time.

7. 'I + X = C' belief creates an *imaginary* void in the beginning itself. One then starts living in a chase mode to fill up that void.

8. Even when the void is temporarily filled up, the understanding that 'there must be a void to be filled up' is not given up. One just keeps running from one object to another all the time.

Where to experience happiness?

When the mind is restful,
peace and happiness is experienced.

When the mind is restless,
excitement or unhappiness is experienced.

One old lady was searching for her lost needle under a pole of light in her street. She could not find it anywhere in the street. One gentleman came and asked her if he could be of some help to her. She explained the situation and now two of them were searching for the lost needle. One hour passed and they could not find it anywhere. Then a wise lady came and offered her help. She asked the old lady where she had dropped the needle. The old lady said that she had dropped it somewhere in her room! Then the wise lady asked her why was she searching for it outside the room, in the street? The old lady said she was doing it because there was no light in her room and there was light in the street!

1. Isn't it absurd? Nay, isn't it unintelligent? Isn't it stupid, this kind of behavior?

2. The search for happiness similarly will be fruitful only when we look for it where we have lost it. *Happiness is a state of*

one's own mind. One cannot find it anywhere outside. People try to find it in their various X factors. It does not exist in any X factor. That is why, most of us here are unhappy.

3. *Happiness is not a transportable or transferable entity*. Money cannot give it to you. Relatives cannot give it to you. Friends cannot give it to you. You only imagine that it will come from them and you start *acting* and *reacting* accordingly. Nothing is being exchanged in reality – only imaginations!

4. There is a spiritual law: *When the mind is restful, peace and happiness is experienced. When the mind is restless, temporary pleasure or unhappiness is experienced*. The actual question is: what is our true requirement – the former or the latter?

5. If your car needs overhauling and you start renovating your house, will it ever help your car? If entity A needs repair, you cannot be working on entity B instead. *It is the mind that needs to be fixed if you want to be happy.* Your trying to fix the world instead is not going to serve any purpose. Your accumulation of wealth or your chasing people are not going to be of any avail. Have you not tried it enough yet?

Illusion of Permanence

Which desire leads to lasting fulfillment?

There was a bull living in a village in India. It used to plough the lands of a poor farmer who would make it slog day in and day out. One day, it prayed to God that it wanted to exchange roles with its master. God listened and immediately fulfilled this desire of the bull. Now, the bull-farmer had to take care of the family as well. It was a big responsibility. His wife was very nagging and demanding. The children were cranky and he had to manage the ruffian landlord of the village as well. The bull-farmer got fed up in seven days only and started praying to God if he could become the landlord of the village. And God fulfilled this desire also.

As the landlord of the village, the responsibilities grew further. He had to report to the king every week and pay him a lot of money to keep him happy. The king was cruel and would kill anybody even for a trivial reason. The bull-landlord got exhausted here also and started praying to God to make him the king. God fulfilled this wish also and made him the king.

The kingship also lasted for a few days only as the responsibilities and headaches grew further. In the end, the bull-king prayed to God to give back to him the peaceful life of a bull!

1. When you think that you need something or somebody or some change in life to be happy, how do you feel? Will you call this feeling a happy feeling? Even if it is, how long does it last?

2. When you are caught up in a desire, do you understand that the result will be temporary and you will be hopping once again in a few days? Do you remember that you were hopping for something else just a few days back?

3. This understanding that happiness will come from somewhere else is at the root of all the suffering. It never comes and you keep chasing.

4. The illusion of permanence: 'If this desire gets fulfilled, it will give me lasting happiness!' What actually happens is that this apparent fulfillment will create new desires and hence, new problems. And it will remain like that forever. You will keep forgetting that even the last time when you were caught in your desire-web, you were thinking similarly.

The future-past mindset

You cannot control the future or past.
You cannot be happy in the future or past.
Happiness always happens in the present.

Susan Claire was in the office taking dictation from her boss Tom. It was 9.30 in the morning and she was already exhausted. She had been living in a strong dilemma about her job. She wanted to discontinue with this work. She strongly desired to go back to school to get her degree for teaching kids. She loved children and wanted to take up teaching as her profession. She believed that she would be happy only in the future when things would change.

As she came out of Tom's room and went to her cabin, she was on the verge of crying: 'How long? How long will it continue?' Susan felt helpless. She could not give up the job as there were many urgent responsibilities on her shoulders. She kept brooding throughout the day, but could not come up with any decision.

1. Is this not the mindset of most of us? Is Susan not living in you too?

2. What are the properties of this kind of a mind:

    a. Dreaming most the time, if not all the time.

b. Desire to change the future or past.

c. Worrying or regretting about the future or past.

d. Inability to live and enjoy the present moment.

e. Helplessness and restlessness.

f. Running in circles, especially when facing a problem.

g. Lack of awareness and fickleness.

3. By trying to control the future or past, one invariably spoils the present. One wants to act God, but one cannot do it in reality. Nobody can do it. As a result, one suffers.

4. If you were in Susan's position, what would you do? Why?

Utility standpoint

Running in circles never take you to your goal. Thoughtfulness may.

Enat had her final exams going on. She had come to US and got admission at Stanford for doing her MBA. She had been studying hard for her exams. But today, it was extremely difficult to concentrate. She was missing her parents who lived in Tel Aviv. She got a call from her mother in the morning. Her mother was not well and she wanted Enat to come back to Israel immediately.

Enat was in front of the book for three hours and she had not turned even a single page. She was continuously revolving around 'Should I go back; should I not....'

1. In the background of the mind of most of us, the unconscious and futile daydreaming continuously goes on. When such daydreaming is happening, one mistakenly takes it to be reality and therefore, one does not remain aware of the reality of the moment. When one is not aware of the reality of the moment, one's efficiency in the moment reduces considerably. What one could have achieved in less time and using less energy, one takes much more time and energy to do that.

2. Enat is, in reality, not moving an inch further toward what she is concerned about. She is doing circles in her mind. She is neither deciding about going back nor studying. She is just confused.

3. Both future and past cannot be touched and controlled by anybody. *One can only take the best possible thoughtful steps living in the present and in the dharmic direction of the future.* This is called thoughtful living in the present and it is very different from trying to control the flow of events in the future or past. The latter invariably saps one's energies.

4. The ideal scenario is: Jot down pros and cons of each solution and take a decision keeping your priorities straight. Whether Enat should go back or not is not the question. The question is 'Why?'.

Rebecca-mind and Happiness

*One cannot not live in the present moment
and be peacefully happy also.*

Rebecca was married to Paul for thirty years. Although, they had spent many happy times together, yet she always carried this grudge in her heart: 'Why doesn't he have words of appreciation for her? Why was it that Paul appeared indifferent at times and even callous sometimes? With everybody else, he was quite positive and loving, but with her, there was something lacking...

1. A Rebecca-mind is considered *normal* even by our psychologists! In this mind, the background is noisy and is full of expectations and desires from others. *These expectations and desires are considered natural by their carriers.*

2. Rebecca-mind has these basic qualities of grasping and rejection. The consequence is suffering which can be in the form of sadness, worries, stress, depression, hopelessness, jealousy, anger, restlessness, boredom, loneliness, dejection, fears or any such unhappy feeling.

3. Even when this mind appears to be happy sometimes, there are these shortcomings:

a. There is lack of control as it keeps dreaming.

b. There is no awareness of the present moment and it still lives in the past or future.

c. Grasping and rejection remain hidden even when one is apparently happy. This can give birth to insecurity and fears about the future.

4. Imagine a state in which future and past have vanished. When one has given up grasping and rejection, what would be the experience like? This experience will be that of unconditioned peace and happiness.

5. Another question is: Do you really want peace and happiness more than desiring and controlling?

For or From?

$$I = C$$

Michel was a publisher of IT books and was quite successful in this field. His employees were very smart and would always keep him ahead of other competitors. He would also take good care of the entire company.

After working hard for fifteen years, Michel started to feel burnt out. Something was missing somewhere in his life. He could not exactly figure out what it was, but he was dissatisfied. He tried to take the help of a counselor, but it did not work.

Then Michel went to India where he met a monk in the Himalayas. He stayed with the monk for three months and learnt the art of de-conditioning the mind and realizing its true nature. As he had a sincere and subtle mind, his practice deepened and after about a year of living in India, he went back to Sydney to publish the IT books again! He lived happily thereafter and helped a lot of people as well!

1. There are only two ways of living in this world:

   a. Live *for* completeness.

   b. Live *from* completeness.

In the first part of his life, Michel was living a good life, as they say it in the common parlance. He had a successful business, a nice wife, beautiful children and a daily list of chores. But, there was little awareness about how his mind operated. It just followed the customary ways of living – believing that happiness came from outside. So he was living in a chase mode and got exhausted eventually.

In the second part, when he became aware of the mind and the conditionings that drive it, he started a process of disillusionment through meditation. Then the entire perspective of living changed. The same job, the same people around, the same chores – but he was now in total control of his life. The fulfillment no longer depended upon the externals. He was now a free man; and hence, a happy man.

2. The second kind of life is for a very few brave ones who dare to walk in the virgin lands. *The illusion that happiness comes from outside is the only obstacle.* In this second scenario, the X factor is dropped and the greatest fulfillment experience of 'I = C' is lived!

Dharma

What is your best possibility?

1. This question is often asked in the Z Meditation Retreats:
    'Now that I have learnt that I just need to work on myself
    and realize a state of unconditioned inner completeness,
    what next? I accept this life in which I live from
    completeness and not for; but what to do after that?'

2. It is very simple now onwards. Once you let go of the
    illusions of duality, reality, permanence and incompleteness,
    once your 'X' factor is dropped and you realize that all the
    fulfillment is already within you, you just have to let your
    dharma shine forth. Dharma in this context means *your
    natural state of being*. It might be physics for an Einstein,
    painting for a Picasso, or writing for a Tagore. It could be
    social service for a Mother Teresa, religion for a Dalai Lama
    and football for a Pele. You just live in your dharma and fill
    up your time with the love for it.

3. That means you are not dependent upon the results of your
    actions anymore. *You follow your dharma with love,
    happiness and awareness. You don't want to win games; you*

just love playing. Your job is to keep tossing the coins of your dharma -- 'Heads or tails' is immaterial for you.

4. In this context, you need to differentiate very thoughtfully between *giving your life a meaningful dharmic direction* and *doing things for some distant fruits.* The latter gives worries. The former is a joyful process. You will still need to have strategies; you will still be busy. But you will not be anxious or stressed about the results of what you do. For you, the means will be the goals.

5. There will of course be problems on the way. But for you, solving them will be like solving sums of mathematics – with equanimity and joy. You will take on things as and when they present themselves to you. You will never have any reason to hurry or worry.

6. Keeping the X factors alive in your life simply means that you have desires and you believe that their fulfillment will give you fulfillment. It never happens. When you get disillusioned from this basic flaw in understanding, your entire life becomes a joyful celebration. Each day of your life is lived with love – love for yourself, love for what you do and love for people around you.

7. Unconditioned happiness and love are the primary dharmas of all human beings. They realize it or not, is a different matter altogether. When this primary dharma shines with the renunciation of desiring, once secondary dharma naturally starts glowing. There will be no reason for such a person to follow any vocation other than his true one.

Three Qualities of Mind

Nothing is to be taken personally.
Everybody here is acting compulsively.

1. How is it that some people are greedy and some are generous? Some are compassionate and some are callous? Some are lazy and some are over-active? Some are contemplative and some flippant? How and why are people different from each other?

2. These differences are natural. There are three inherent qualities of the mind. As liquidity, transparency and wetness are to water, as heat and light are to the Sun, these three inherent qualities are to the mind – all human minds.

3. The child does not leave the womb with a clean chit. Its mind has inbuilt properties which manifest with age.

4. The first quality is *Lethargy* with *confusion* as its main attribute.

5. The second is *Sensuality* with *dependence on sensual objects* as its main feature.

6. The third is *Integrity* with *knowledge and happiness* as its main traits.

7. Everybody has all these three qualities. You cannot find anybody in this world who can say that he has one more or one less.

8. Still people differ in their behavior. That is because the proportion of the three qualities is different in each one. People can be lethargic, sensual or integrated depending on the preponderance of the respective quality. It is not that a lethargic person will not have sensuality or integrity at all. It is just that he will be predominantly lethargic. And the same with the other two.

9. Let us study the three qualities with three *real* examples.

   a. Sam, the lethargic.

   b. Tom and Sarah, the sensuals.

   c. Mark, the integrated.

Sam's lethargic patterns

Never ever give an uncalled for advice.
Especially to a congenital whiner.

1. Sam and his wife Shrutz live in this world! One day, Sam had to pick up his wife at the airport. She was coming back from a meditation retreat of seven days. On their way back, they found out that there was no gas in their car and they got stuck in the middle of a freeway.

   Sam was very unhappy with Shrutz: 'She should have paid more attention and reminded him the day before about filling up the tank.' He was yelling throughout the day, blaming her for what had happened. And this was not the first time.

2. Sam and Shrutz went for a picnic with their two children. He was driving the car as he knew the way to the picnic spot on the beach. It so happened that he lost the way and had to drive back for about fifteen miles. Shrutz had dozed off when this happened. Then suddenly, she was woken up by her ever-unhappy husband who was again blaming her that it was because she had slept that they lost the way. He was now driving back home in anger!

3. Sam needs about twelve hours of sleep everyday and in his waking time, he either watches football or chats with his friends on telephone or internet. He runs the household by the income from renting his properties. Shrutz's income and the rental income are barely sufficient for their family, but that is never a concern for Sam.

4. Sam gets very angry if anyone gives him advice – especially Shrutz.

5. Sam has grand projects of earning millions of dollars in a short time. He just keeps inventing and living in his fancies and never puts anything to practice. The moment something is done to bring about direction in his life, he feels morose or angry.

6. If Shrutz asks him to search for a job, she becomes his biggest enemy. He sometimes threatens her that he will commit suicide if she keeps pestering him to find a job.

7. If Sam gives an opinion and you support him on that, he can instantly reject it and start advocating a different one. He really feels from his heart that he knows the best and most others are fools. Especially Shrutz!

8. If a problem is there, he gets nervous and looks toward Shrutz to bring him out of the mess he so often creates. After taking her help, he is never grateful. He never acknowledges the fact that sometimes others can also be right.

9. When he takes out his clothes from the closet, he spoils the entire stack and does not understand that he is creating unnecessary trouble for others. It takes Shrutz a lot of time to mend what he does.

10. He often broods and laments that his mother did not allow him to join the Army twenty years before. He feels he would have excelled there.

11. Sam does not like discipline. He likes freedom!

12. He does not normally do things in time. He always feels that it can happen better the next day, as he would get more time to think. The next day, he needs some more time to think. It goes on and on. And when he cannot postpone anymore and has to take solid steps, he does it half-heartedly as if it is a big load of work that he has to finish.

13. You mostly see him saying that he does not have time. His life is too busy. And in reality, he does nothing!

14. When he is sick, he becomes like a child. He needs all attention and care. But when the children or Shrutz are sick, he hardly pays any attention. He is very busy, especially during those times.

15. He is never happy with his neighbors. He feels that they are all selfish and he should always keep his defenses up.

Lethargy

'Confusion' is from nature, not from individuals.
Why get upset?

1. In a lethargic person, confusion reigns supreme in the mind. He cannot easily draw inferences and conclusions. Given a cause, what could be the effect and given an effect, what were the possible causes – he cannot think along these lines.

2. He mostly remains indecisive. He runs in circles of vagueness and triviality. If he has to face a problem, he does not think about the possible solutions. He just revolves around 'I have a problem…. I have a problem'. He cannot weigh in terms of 'pros and cons'. He cannot even try to think about the consequences of his actions.

3. He does not and cannot gauge his potential and has great pride for his extraordinary abilities!

4. His fears and worries are all baseless. He could be scared that he would be run over by a car or would dash against a tree suddenly!

5. He is fickle-minded to the extreme. Even in a short conversation, you can see him jumping and changing his views very quickly.

6. He lives mostly in the past and is mostly unhappy about it. He often has these lethargic feelings of sadness, regret, guilt, jealousy, lamentation, grief, depression etc. These feelings are putrefying as they don't let you move on.

7. His life does not have anything to look forward to. That is, he does not have ambitions and goals to achieve. His mind has countless incoherent thoughts and he is always lost in them. There is *no* possibility of his coming out of this jungle.

8. He often has severe mood swings.

9. His room and closet are always disorganized – just like his mind and life.

10. He procrastinates everything. Today is never a good day for him to take necessary steps.

11. He can be creative in lying and finding excuses. He is irresponsible in his jobs. His undertakings are unsteady. His work is shoddy and clearly smells of thoughtlessness.

12. He is insensitive in relationship. He can be very callous toward others' feelings.

13. He never owns responsibility. He always blames and criticizes and holds others responsible for his unhappiness and failure.

14. He can be foolishly stubborn at times.

15. He despises listening to others. In extreme cases of lethargy, he can be malicious, quarrelsome, abusive and cruel also.

16. The X factor of a lethargic person can be alcohol, drugs, viewing television for hours at a stretch, gossiping, over-sleeping etc. That is, he takes resort to lazy means to get away from the chaos of his mind.

17. It is not just individuals, even nations can be lethargic. When you see broken roads not being repaired, crisscrossing electric wires, corruption & bribery in administration, shoddy jobs, people having lot of time for fruitless gossiping and inability to accept positive criticism & advice, you can easily make out that these people are predominantly lethargic.

Sarah and Tom's hectic life style

For meditation, leisure is necessary.

1. Tom gets up at six in the morning. He wakes up his children
    and prepares them for going to school. His wife Sarah leaves
    home earlier. Her work starts at seven.
    Tom leaves at 7.30. Drives twenty miles to first reach the
    day-care of his two-year-old son. Dropping him there, he
    goes to his daughter's school and then to his office around
    8.30. He reaches late by a few minutes almost daily.

2. He leaves office at 5.25 in the evening and picks up his
    children. By the time he reaches home, it is 7 o'clock. He
    watches television and plays with his children for some time.
    He brings home his office daily. He goes to sleep around
    11.00.

3. In the evening, Sarah prepares dinner and gives her children
    the evening shower and she retires around 9.30.

4.   The weekends are always packed for both of them. They do
    shopping, laundry, dishes and cleaning on Saturdays. And on
    Sundays, they go out either for a party or to a movie.
    Sometimes, they invite or are invited by friends.

5. Both Tom and Sarah have many desires from life and from each other. Sarah wants to see her husband become the CEO of a big company.

6. Tom and Sarah want to have a lot of money. They like traveling to exotic locations. In the last ten years, they have changed three houses and three cars.

7. When some desires are fulfilled or when they are enjoying with friends, they are happy. When they are at home, they are neither happy nor unhappy. They just follow their routines.

8. Tom and Sarah have family-oriented minds – everything for their own families only. The outsiders don't form a part of their thinking. They sometimes visit their parents.

9. They can go on living this life until they have to finally retire. They look forward to the days when they will be able to relax.

Sensuality

They manufacture tension in the X factory.

1. A sensual person feels that the objects of the senses are the only reality; happiness is dependent on sense pleasures; desires must be there and their fulfillment is the goal of life. He says: 'Eat, drink and enjoy – this is the best philosophy.'

2. He feels: 'To fulfill these desires, one should work hard. One should spend most of one's time in working to earn a lot of money.'

3. The X factory of a sensual person consists of money, sex, relationships, power, status, superiority, praise, approval from others, gadgets, cars, houses etc.

4. 'My wife and my children' – this is his world.

5. Desires fulfilling, he throws parties. If there are obstacles on the way, he is morose.

6. He has always a desire for *more*: more money, bigger car, bigger house, new travel destinations. His life is about making it big.

7. Clear strategy, perfect planning and relentless execution – this is his way. But he does it only for his desires!

8. His inferences and conclusions are clear and help him fulfill his desires. Manipulations and calculations to beat others are positive for him.

9. A sensual person lives mostly in the future and is habitually stressed about it.

10. He has a lot many expectations from people around him. He himself may not happily do what he expects others to do.

11. He sometimes gets excited by patriotic feelings also. But they don't last long.

12. He has many ambitions and goals. And the fulfillment of his desires never fulfills him. He loves to begin new activities as his desires are countless.

13. 'Peace and Compassion should be practiced when one is old' – he feels. 'Those who cannot do anything, only they meditate' – he thinks.

14. He suffers from stressful feelings like greed, anger, pride, lust and attachment. These feelings goad him to move on and on.

15. His vacations are spent in exotic locations. It is more for temporary relief that he goes to these places. He needs a different place each time.

16. If he ever donates, he does it for recognition or for some other ulterior motive.

17. He likes to eat pungent and hot things. He needs a lot of variety in food. He loves to go to a new restaurant every time he goes out for dinner.

18. Between 'pleasant' and 'good', he would prefer the former. He cannot wait. He hardly has patience. He is impulsive at times.

19. He cannot understand that discontentment is not happiness; chasing is not reaching and stress is not good for his health. He just cannot as he is too busy to think.

Mark Wellhams' Integrity

Mindfulness is a pre-requisite for fulfillment.

1. Mark lives in Holland. Alone but never lonely. He works part-time for an NGO that helps seniors. He loves his job and looks forward to going to work every day.

2. His day begins at 5.30. After his morning ablutions – clearing the bowels is a must for him – he meditates for two hours and tries to experience the blissful silence within. He understands that unless one lets go of the societal programming, one cannot be peaceful. Peace, fulfillment and love are what he cherishes and guards with utmost care.

3. Mark believes that unless one clears the mind with meditation in the morning, it is difficult to remain aware and peaceful during the rest of the day. He finishes his meditation with a resolve to carry it to the rest of the day.

4. He leaves at 9.45 for his work. His office is just ten minutes walk from home. This gives him a good meditative bridge from home to office as he walks mindfully to office. From office, he needs to go to various old-age homes to help the seniors there. He consciously sees to it that he remains calm and compassionate throughout the day.

5. He comes back home at 3.30 in the afternoon. Then is the time for mindfully preparing his lunch and eating it with awareness and gratitude.

6. Mark must take a nap of at least half-an-hour in the afternoon as he wants to feel fresh for his evening meditation. From five o'clock, he sits for meditation – releasing the futile programs and realizing stillness of the Self. He believes that unless one practices regularly and systematically, it is difficult to get rid of the inner turmoil.

7. He sometimes watches spiritual programs on television and sometimes studies scriptures. This is like tonic for his soul. He has his evening eating meditation of salads and fruits around 9.00. Sometimes, Mark watches programs on Discovery channel.

8. Before going to sleep at 11.00, he sits for the last doze of meditation for fifteen minutes. When he is on his back on the bed, he keeps practicing meditation until he falls asleep.

9. On weekends, Mark visits his parents. He also goes to a monastery to meet his community and listen to the discourses. He likes to remain at home on Sundays and just relax, and meditate, and walk, and visit a park to see children playing.

10. Once in a while, Mark goes to a National Park to be with the trees. He loves walking in the forest.

11. Mark does not want to get married. But he is open to having a like-minded companion.

12. As far as he can, he practices living in the moment with awareness, happiness and love.

13. Mark's vacations are mostly spent in India. He goes to his favorite retreat for three weeks every year. Seeing new places is not his way of traveling.

Integrity

The present moment is the best present.
The grass is the greenest right under the nose.

1. A person with fully-blossomed integrity clearly knows that the present moment must be lived in fulfillment as nothing else is real. Worries of the future or regrets about the past do not make a part of his mind.

2. As his mind is peaceful with regard to the imaginations and turmoil about past and future, he can easily come to right conclusions and one-pointed decisions. He is never fickle-minded as he understands that it serves no purpose to dilly-dally.

3. He may take his time in thinking about the possibilities in a given problem, but once he is clear and has taken a stand, he sticks to his guns whatever the general opinion is.

4. His means are his ends. Doing things with awareness, love and happiness is what he likes. His undertakings are full of compassionate purpose. He never wavers from his dharma.

5. His priorities are clear and he lives accordingly.

6. In his meditation, he easily attains stillness and bliss. In his interactions, he easily practices unconditioned loving kindness.

7. His needs are limited and he hardly has any wants. His sense organs are satisfied and he does not care for what others think about him. Between peace and excitement, he always goes for peace. Nothing is more important than peace; but for a right cause, he does not mind getting into hectic activity also.

8. He does not appreciate the imaginary boundaries of nationality, language, religion, sex, family and wealth etc. For him, whosoever is in front is worthy of respect and love. Even plants and animals receive unconditioned love from him.

9. His life is happily disciplined. He does not like to experiment with new things or programs. He would rather go for the proven methods to achieve his inner goals.

The ladder of evolution

Dissatisfaction has a beautiful silver lining:
You start growing.

1. To understand the mind's needs still better, let us now study the ladder of evolution. This will give you an idea about how it evolves. The tangible criteria of evolution are peace and loving kindness – the realization of the absolute is its ultimate possibility.

2. At the lowest rung of the ladder of human evolution, you see turmoil and confusion. That is a *lethargic mind* whose qualities have been enumerated in detail earlier. Disorder, chaos, running in circles, indecisiveness, procrastination, aimless living, baseless fears and worries, blaming, criticizing, jealousy, guilt, hatred, un-quenchable remorse, mood swings and in extreme cases, viciousness are the traits of lethargy. One takes resort to alcohol, drugs, television and useless gossiping etc. to run away from the inner noise; but nothing gives satisfaction for more than a few hours.

3. *When dissatisfaction takes place with one's current state of being, one moves up on the ladder of evolution.* If one is satisfied with the current ways of thinking and living, there is

no reason that one will like to move up. *It is also not necessary that the movement must take place in everybody's life.* In most cases, one lifetime is too short a time to outgrow the current state of being.

4. The lethargic X factors give a very-very short term relief from the turmoil of one's mind. In using these X factors, there is the facility of ease, but there is the difficulty that they don't serve the purpose of lasting fulfillment. The fulfillment coming from them is as transient as a bubble.

5. The next state is the *sensual state*. The X factory of sensuality consists of sensual pleasures, power, ambitions and relentless activity. This has also been discussed before. A sensual person has many desires and expectations and he always lives in hopes and fears related to the future. He does get some pleasure and excitement, but this is also transient. The price he pays for it is enormous. He is never peaceful and happy. His life is a continuous struggle for attaining, achieving and accumulating. He lives in a state of stress all the time.

6. Some get fed up with this life-style and decide to take the next step which is toward the *aesthetic-creative* state of consciousness. Now, some subtlety starts coming in life.

One's attention and love turns towards the *intelligence type(s)* one is strong in. It means one revels in one's natural secondary dharma grooves. These are the six intelligence types created by nature:

a. Linguistic: Love for fiction, non-fiction, philosophy, oratory, poetry etc.

b. Mathematical-logical: Love for the natural sciences, mathematics, modern philosophy, statistics etc.

c. Musical: Love for music – vocal and / or instrumental.

d. Kinesthetic: Love for sports, yoga, swimming, athletics etc.

e. Spatial: Love for colors and space as you see in architects, designers, sculptors etc.

f. Intra-personal: Love for psychology, psychotherapy and related fields.

7. The aesthetic-creative state is the first step in bringing about some integrity in the mind. Now one's concentration and stability grow. Even the duration and quality of happiness become better. Somebody in this state will love studying fiction or non-fiction, going to operas & classic movies, spending evenings in swimming pools or football grounds,

dancing, music, painting or similar pursuits. One experiences a lot of joy in following one's favorite activity.

8. However, when one is not doing what one likes doing, one is either bored or just drags on. The creativity has a shadow aspect of pride also – I-know-the-best attitude. Many creatives live unhappy lives as they are emotionally very sensitive and don't know how to balance the feelings with understanding. The application of creativity for uplifting one's consciousness is a different game altogether.

9. The next milestone is the state of compassion in which one understands that without opening the heart, something will always remain missing. The attachment with an intelligence type gets sublimated into attachment with a cause. For example, it is just not physics that remains a motivating factor; it will rather be love of humanity for which physics will be studied. Not just music, but its soothing and enlivening effects on the listeners become a driving force. Selfless love becomes important now and one consciously takes steps to develop it.

10. No doubt, it is beautiful to have a compassionate heart, but it has its own limitations:

a. A compassionate person is passionate about a cause; but if he does not achieve the desired results, he gets put off easily. He is still too dependent on success and failure. He might not be doing things for any selfish ends, but even this selflessness can become a cause of pain. He wants to bring about *quick* and *lasting* changes in the society – and this is a hopeless desire.

b. He gets burnt out with time. In our meditation retreats, most of our students belong to this state of consciousness. What beautiful hearts they have! Many of them come to India just to do some volunteer work, just to give some comfort to the suffering humanity. Yet we have seldom met anybody who is peaceful just because he is compassionate. Lasting peace requires something more.

c. Sensitivity of a compassionate person also affects him in his interactions with others. He easily gets disturbed by what others think about him. He does not know the art of balancing his feelings with his understanding.

11. There comes a time in the life of a compassionate person when he starts searching for some more enriching avenues. The next step is the state of *introspection* in which the mind turns inwards and starts asking questions about the nature

of the self, the causes of unhappiness, the way to peace etc. One starts inquiring as to what is real and unreal; what is the source of all that appears to the senses – the whence and whither of the universe. This inquiry takes one to the most important question that one can ever ask oneself: *"Who am I?"* It is a long journey before one can deserve asking this supreme question, but when the ripe time comes, meditation begins.

12. The process of evolution within the state of introspection can be slightly different for each person; but essentially, it takes this shape:

a. Studying self-help books to learn how to become strong in mind and how to have better concentration.

b. Turning toward spiritual texts or places or teachers to understand more about the inner-growth possibilities.

c. Practicing meditation, which is more of a concentration practice in the beginning.

d. One may follow any of the three main paths of meditation – the path of knowledge, devotion or awareness. All of them lead to the same goal. It all depends upon one's natural tendencies.

e. In the initial stages, there is hardly any integration of the study with one's real life. There is dichotomy in theory and practice and one is still lost in the illusions of duality, reality, permanence and incompleteness. One has a vague understanding about the true purpose of meditation, but one is not able to live up to it.

f. Slowly, one recognizes that it is not possible to quiet the mind in meditation unless these concepts are also lived in day-to-day life. It means one makes the following efforts and eventually realizes their fruition:

- Experiencing fulfillment within oneself – independent of X factors.

- Living in awareness, peace and love each moment.

- Helping others without expectations.

- Faith in the teachings.

- Happy acceptance of people as they are.

- Learning to benefit from the difficulties.

- Considering fulfillment more important than excitement.

- Considering purity more important than lust.

- Considering peace more important than anger.

- Considering detachment more important than attachment.

- Considering contentment more important than greed.

- Considering humility more important than pride.

- Non-interference in the business of others.

- Not blaming and criticizing others.

- Loving oneself in peace and in one's own dharma.

g. As one progresses in meditation, one realizes that the *notion of possession is only a dream*. 'That this house or money or person is mine' is the cause of so much agitation. The sense of possession leads to desires, fears and insecurities. They, in turn, cause the initiation of many activities. One just keeps running all the time due to these false imaginations!

h. Proceeding further in this inner journey of meditation, *the idea that 'I am this body-mind complex' is also shaken up.* Initially, it comes only for a short duration, but with practice, the duration of experiencing one's true identity with the *'eternal blissful awareness'* becomes much more concrete.

i. As this experience deepens further, one truly sees that one is the eternal Self – blissful awareness. This experience matures with practice. At first, there is an oscillatory movement between remembrance and forgetting. With practice, one gets established in the Self as the only reality.

13. Until the experience of one's identity with the eternal blissful awareness becomes stable, it is called the state of introspection. When vacillation and forgetfulness cease completely, and there takes place continuity in experiencing the Self, it is called the *state of Self Establishment*. One becomes stable in the understanding and experience of one's identity with the Self – the eternal blissful awareness. It is no longer a far off concept. It is one's true identity. One realizes that one is self-luminous – there was never a time when one was not and there will never be a time when one will be not. Coming into being and ceasing to be does not happen in the reality of the Self – these are just notions of the mind.

14. This remarkable realization brings about a complete change in the perception of the reality. The world, with all its concepts, conditionings and relationships, becomes a non-entity. It is seen to be a long dream, rooted only in wrong notions.

15. There is no coming back into the darkness of ignorance from here.

16. Now, there is only one more step to be taken and then one is called Enlightened – which is the state of Liberation. Here, the small wave merges back into the infinite ocean! The notion that 'one is a separate Self' is give up when the experience of union with the Cosmic Self takes place. One realizes that there is only one reality that has superimposed upon itself infinite names, forms and qualities. *It means that the three-fold differentiation between the knower, the known and the knowledge gets annihilated now. Only One remains. It is the experience of the Universal Consciousness, Blissful and Eternally Aware. 'I am the Self' gets sublimated into 'I am not; only That is'. Total and unequivocal surrender takes place. One always lives in non-forgetfulness of the Truth.*

17. This is the ladder of evolution. You will see that on the lowest rung of lethargy, there is total chaos and confusion and on the highest, there is the purest awareness and bliss. In between, there are steps for growing. One very important fact is that *it is not possible to omit the steps*. It is just not possible for a lethargic or sensual mind to straightaway jump

to the state of liberation. One has to pass through and outgrow the steps on the way.

18. What is however possible is that one can expedite the process by bringing in conscious intensity, sincerity and perseverance.

19. It is often seen is that people find themselves oscillating between lethargy and introspection. They do like spirituality, but they have their strong tendencies also. They don't want to give them up in the beginning. It shows that they have a good potential for spiritual life, but they are not serious enough for their growth. What they need to do is that they must spend most of their time in their higher states of being. They should try to meditate more deeply and clear all the doubts. The sooner one realizes that one's true and lasting fulfillment resides within oneself, the better. Otherwise, how can one grow on a foundation of illusions?

20. There are only two paths for the inner growth:

a. **Natural evolution**: You go through various experiences – good and bad – and slowly learn from them. The so-called bad experiences give you detachment and the so-called good experiences lead to attachment. You oscillate between them and learn your lessons slowly. It takes you a long time to understand that happiness resides within you.

b. **Revolutionary evolution**: You contemplate, meditate and thereby outgrow illusions and desires. It involves clear understanding, deep honesty and indomitable courage.

21. There is an ancient story of two birds, Sam and Peter. They used to live on two different branches of a tree. Sam was living on the lowest branch and Peter was on the highest. Sam was ever dissatisfied with life. It used to be discontented with the quality of fruits that came on the tree – the fruits of the other trees were better. It always felt that others were living better and happier lives. And Peter – it was ever serene and fulfilled; always indrawn and full of gratitude.

Sam's life was full of happenings. If it ate a bitter fruit, it would feel bad and would look up to its friend Peter who was always happy. It would think in those moments of distress how peaceful and contented its friend was. There always arose a desire to be like Peter and then it would jump up to the next higher branch. On that branch it would look for fruits again. On eating a sweet fruit, it would ask for more and more of sweet fruits. But on eating bitter fruits, the suffering made Sam move up to the next higher branch. Slowly and slowly, after many years of eating sweet and bitter fruits, Sam reached the highest branch of the tree and a miracle happened there...

Sam merged into Peter! It realized that it was ever one with its friend. The distance was just an imagination. They were actually one.

22. Yes, the distance is imaginary. Your highest possibility is a state of your mind. You are only postponing its realization by holding on to various illusions. You are one with Buddha, Christ and Krishna. Just accept it and start living. If you cannot, you may have to consume many bitter fruits in life. The choice is yours. If you want to go through the tedious and long process of natural evolution because your desires are too strong, it is perfectly fine; but you must keep in mind the consequences. You should not blame anybody else later on. If you think that you can get true happiness from the external world of senses, just try; and keep trying. There is going to come a day in your life when you will yourself shun this illusion as poison.

23. Normally, there does not occur much change in the life of an unconscious person. Unless one is *consciously working* to

outgrow one's given character-patterns, one just dies with the same mindset that one was born with.

24. However, *if one wants to hit the target without delay, meditation is the only way*. Sincere and systematic practice of right understanding is the master key to this problem of suffering.

Why is it difficult to meditate?

Lethargics and sensuals cannot understand meditation. For others, success depends upon honesty.

Vijayashree is a funny character. I know her for many years. She tells everybody that she is very happy, but wants to poke her nose in everybody's affairs! She thinks that God has been gracious to her, but also has endless desires! She believes that she accepts people with love, but gets disturbed just on the drop of a hat! She feels that she does not care what others are thinking about her, but wants to talk about herself even with strangers! When you try to tell her that she is hooked to so many things and if she wants to be happy, she has to unhook herself, she immediately becomes defensive and tells you that she is already unhooked and detached from everything!

Shambhavi is also a normal human being. She did the Z Meditation retreat a few years before. At that time, she appeared very jovial and carefree. She told me that she had no desires left, except one – she wanted to live in a big house with about ten thousand square feet area! She was then living in an apartment, which was not suitable to her high standards! During the retreat, she said that she was very peaceful and did not have even one disturbing thought to work on!

A few years later, her only desire got fulfilled. Her husband bought her a big house in the locality where she wanted to live. But things had changed dramatically by then. She did not want that house anymore! The reason for coming to the retreat again was that her relationship with her husband was acrimonious and she wanted to get divorce! She had only this desire left – this time!

1. What I understand here is that even during her first retreat, she had countless disturbing thoughts – as her basic character was sensual. The sensuals and lethargics are always restless; never peaceful. But they are so lost that they cannot understand and see that they are lost.

2. When one is happily attached to the mind's qualities, it is extremely difficult to work on it. Most of the people in our world – more than 99% -- are like that. For them, the illusion of incompleteness is not an illusion. They really and truly feel that they would get their happiness through the desire-fulfillment route. They are not in a position to even listen to the truth. Hence, it is difficult – almost impossible – for them to internalize the gaze and meditate.

True Meaning of Laziness

The distance is just in your mind.
Just Accept and Be.

Zen Master Blumise was growing very old. He had been the head abbot of No Wind Monastery for a very long time and was ready to anoint a successor. Master Blumise decreed that the monk who he felt was least lazy, would take over as head abbot of No Wind Monastery. Everyone knew that the real competition was only between Chin and Tara. They both had immense character, were flush with noble qualities and were favorite students of Master Blumise. The competition was on.

Chin pondered hard as to how he would demonstrate his non-lazy character to Master Blumise and finally came up with a huge list of items that needed to be done around the monastery grounds. This he thought would be appropriate. There was much work to be done and, in accordance with the Zen teachings of physical labor, he would show Master Blumise just how devoted to work he could be. Moreover, Chin knew that some of this work was very physical in nature and that Tara, being a lady of slight stature and build, would not be able to do it even if she decided to. Feeling confident in his plan, he set out to execute it.

Chin began rebuilding the temple roof which had begun to decay. Also, high up on the roof he knew he would be very visible to everyone in the grounds, especially Master Blumise. As he toiled in the hot sun, he noticed Tara far away sitting by the river under a shaded tree. He smiled and mentally awarded himself a point. Early the next morning, Chin sprang out of bed and headed to the monastery kitchen, which he had decided to repaint. Along the way he noticed Tara, awake, but still in bed. "That's 2 points for me," he thought as his smile grew wider.

And so it went. Chin pounding away making the monastery the 8th wonder of the world and Tara strolling along the river, hanging out in bed, drinking tea with her friends and watching the clouds roll by. A week passed and then there was great excitement around the monastery. Master Blumise had made his decision and all had been asked to convene in the newly built Great Meditation Hall.

"My most beloved students," Master Blumise began, "First, I would like to say that we are renaming the Great Meditation Hall to Chin Meditation Hall, to show our collective *appreciation to young Master Chin for rebuilding it so finely and also, for all the terrific work he has done around the monastery grounds." After the sound of one hand clapping settled down, Master Blumise continued, "Master Tara will take over as the head abbot as I am retiring and heading to Disney Land." All were pleased and applauded once more, except of course a confused Chin.*

Later that day, Chin visited Master Blumise and inquired about why he had selected Tara as the least lazy student. "Dearest Chin," said Master Blumise with a soft, compassionate smile, "It was a no-brainer. In the past week she has not let a single thought, emotion or action of hers go unnoticed. She is equal to Shakyamuni Buddha himself in her awareness. I bow to her greatness." Chin understood clearly and bowed as well in admiration and respect.

Laws of Peace

Respect nature and it will love you.

1. Imagine somebody jumping from the fiftieth storey of a building because he believes that he can flout gravity!

2. Imagine somebody putting her bare hands in fire because she believes that she can defy fire!

3. Imagine somebody running his car without gas, as he believes that he can resist friction!

4. You can very well imagine what will happen in all these three cases. The moral of the stories is that it is not possible to challenge the laws of nature. You can invent things like airplanes and fireproof gloves etc., but they also follow certain other laws of nature. Nature is supreme. You have to use it intelligently. If you abuse it in any way, you will have to pay the price.

5. The same is true for the internal nature of humans. If you want to be happy, you need to follow certain laws. *Happiness and peace of mind are governed by laws.* If you follow them wisely, you will live peacefully; but if you abuse them in any way, suffering will result.

6. It means that *happiness and peace need to be learnt*. You may not be born with them. You are surely brought up with many conditionings, which generally go against the eternal peace principles. You need to learn and apply these principles in order to annul the damaging effects of these societal and congenital beliefs.

7. Spirituality is an objective science. If you follow its laws, you will live in happiness. If you don't, you will live in suffering and restlessness. The closer we live to these laws, the more peaceful we become. Let us now study the seven laws of peace.

First law of peace

What is is.

1. It was Adi from Israel doing her third meditation retreat with us. She had been struggling with 'Why did my boyfriend leave me?' It was very hard for her to accept that a relationship of nine years could end like that. She felt that it was not due to any fault of hers. Eyal had suddenly got attracted to somebody else and was no longer in love with her. She was also wondering if it really was a sudden happening.

2. What were Adi's possible choices?

a. Eyal living with her new girlfriend + Adi upset and grieving.

b. Eyal realizing his mistake, apologizing, coming back + happy life ever after!

c. Adi accepting the change in Eyal as 'a way of life' + Eyal gone from her life.

3. Adi and Eyal had already discussed it at length and then decided to split up. So the second possibility was not possible at all. That means Adi was left with two choices only – the first and the third. In both the scenarios, Eyal is

gone. But in the first, there is suffering and in the third, there is peace. What would any sane person do if she does not want to suffer?

4. She might say that life is not mathematics. I understand that, but I will still ask her again: 'What choices do you have?'

5. Nature is playing her marvelous game in which coming into being, growth, decay and death are unchangeable occurrences. It happens with relationships also. It happens with everything that has a name and form. If you accept it, you live in peace. If you resist, you live in pain. But your living in pain does not stop nature from following her ways.

6. Nature has strewn such beautiful qualities all around us. These five elements, these sense organs, these sense objects, these minds with lethargy, sensuality and integrity, these mountains, these rivers, these big egos, these compassionate hearts, these greedy minds, these pleasures, these pains.... the list is endless. Everything here is a marvel – if you are not seeing, you must be blind. You must be blinded by your ego, your desires, your attachments and your dependence. When the mind is thus turbulent, it cannot enjoy the marvels as it is too attached, and too

wavering, and too restless. When it is detached, it can attain pure awareness of the marvelous happenings all around. Then betrayal will not be frowned upon; it will rather be looked at with non-interference, wonderment and peace.

7. What is, is. What was, was. What will be, will be. 'I wish it were different' means suffering. Expectations mean chaos. *If it is not mathematics, it is painful.*

8. One student told me once that these three simple words had brought about the biggest change in his life! He learnt to live only after learning this law of peace: What is, is!

Second law of peace

Acceptance is the most delightful living.

1. Adi's third choice is the only one that will give her peace. Her options are simple – acceptance or non-acceptance. If she accepts that it is possible that people can change and it can happen in her life also, things smoothen off. If she doesn't, it is very-very painful.

2. Even from a utilitarian standpoint, what is the choice? One can be peaceful on accepting or one can suffer on non-accepting. And especially when one cannot undo the happening. It is *either-or situation* in most such cases.

3. 'Relationship' is a notion and its various definitions vis a vis various people in our life are nice but mostly wrong. Love, friendship, parenthood and all such similar notions are pre-defined in very rosy terms. When the reality does not match these definitions, suffering takes place. *This mismatch between reality and notions is called pain.*

4. If you want to have peace of mind, you will need to accept these in your life – as they are; without ifs' and buts'.

a. *Three qualities of mind* – People are what they are. They are helplessly following their root character-patterns.

b. *Past and future* – Past exists only in one's transient mental formations – one's memory. Future cannot be known or controlled by anybody. Unconscious dwelling in them always spoils the present by causing distress and worries. We cannot control the fruits of our actions also. The only thing we can control is how we are acting and reacting in this present moment. We *can* choose to live in awareness, love and happiness – that is very much within our domain.

c. *The present circumstances* –This present moment is our opportunity to grow in detachment, fulfillment, understanding and love. Why miss it? If it is a difficult situation, we need to make full use of it for learning detachment, strengthening our endurance and growing spiritually. Peace needs to be learnt. One may not be born with it, but one can certainly study and practice for growing in peace.

d. The inevitable: One spiritual master was asked by his students why he never felt unhappy. He answered, 'unhappiness is a direct result of non acceptance of change. One who could accept change could never be unhappy.'

People will change; the amount of money we have will change; status will change, everybody will get old; beauty will never remain. One who is ever ready and alert about acceptance can never be unhappy. He will rather be aware and peaceful.

e. The necessary: What ought to be done, what is obligatory in the given circumstances and what is the righteous course of action has to be freed from the clutches of dilemmas. Things might be unpleasant, but if they are right then there ought to be no vacillation in execution.

Third law of peace

Resistance is pain.

1. Adi was initially resisting the reality, but she was sincerely
    looking for a way to come out of her pain. In the end, as
    resistance waned, peace and freedom were experienced.
    She realized that she was actually not attached to Eyal. She
    was attached to a state of fulfillment, which she thought
    would come from him. As this illusion was dropped, she
    regained the awareness that she was already fulfilled. She
    was mistakenly identifying it with Eyal.

2. Resistance to the reality is resistance to nature. We are
    supposed to understand that an apple will never taste like a
    mango and an eggplant will never taste like beans. They are
    different. They are just different. Without interfering in the
    nature of apple, we have to learn to enjoy it as it is. Lethargy
    always has the bitter smell of confusion and chaos;
    sensuality must result in greed, attachment and pain; friends
    may not be considerate all the time; love may not get
    reciprocated always. Accepting all possibilities will lead to
    peace. Resistance to the inevitable will always be painful.

3. A question is often asked, 'What about injustice? Should we accept that too and do nothing against it?' I think that this question comes from a poor understanding of the concept of acceptance. Just think if the same injustice is done to you. Would you accept it with equanimity or would you fight against it? Even if you are able to accept it for yourself with peace, how can you expect others to have the same understanding as yourself? They feel pain and your practice of compassion requires that you work for alleviating their pain. The important thing is that whatever steps you take, you do it with equanimity and without imposing the outcome. Just do it with love and for love.

4. A question was once asked by a student, 'Why did Gandhi fight the injustice being perpetrated by the British? Why didn't he accept it peacefully?'
Here we need to see whether the actions are happening for a state of completeness or from a state of completeness. Everybody around Gandhi was living in a mindset that unless the British left the country, they could not be happy. But for Gandhi, living from a state of completeness, the means were the ends. Following his dharma – righteous politics – with equanimity, love and peace was an end in itself.
The destination is living in freedom and not reaching out to freedom.

92

The beauty called 'Problems of life'

Problems are good.

1. Another question is often asked: What about the problems of life? How should we handle them in the light of this teaching? Listen to a story...

There was a devotee of God whose only desire in life was to meet God. He loved God more than anybody else – even more than himself. God was naturally very happy with this devotee.

One day God decided to pay him a visit. Early in the morning, there was a knock at the door of the devotee. He opened the door and saw God standing in front. His eyes were filled with tears of joy. He started dancing and singing hymns in praise of God. God kept His eyes close and listened to him with rapt attention. He was spellbound, seeing this devotion; this love.

After some time, God had to leave and before leaving God requested him to ask for a boon. The devotee said that his only desire of meeting God was already fulfilled. He did not want anything. But if God wanted to give him something, he just wanted that he should not have any more desires and he should always follow God's commands. God said, 'I am very pleased with you. Your desire will be fulfilled.'

As God came out of his house, the devotee caught hold of His hand and asked Him to give the first command. God showed him a big rock in front of his house and asked him to push it. God disappeared now and the devotee went to the rock and started pushing it. Not only for that day, he started pushing the rock every day – from morning till evening. This became his daily worship of God – following His command to the letter and spirit.

This went on for a few months and he was feeling strong and happy.

However, the villagers did not understand him at all. They were very doubtful about his vision of God and asked him to prove it. He further asked him why that rock was not moving at all even after months of pushing. The devotee prayed to God to help him. Everyday he would pray to God to come for help. But God didn't come. One day, out of total disgust, he decided that he would not push the rock anymore.

That night, God appeared to him in a dream and asked him why he gave up pushing the rock. He said that it was not moving and he did not understand the benefit of the whole exercise. He then asked God to explain the benefit.

God said, 'What do you understand by a benefit? Don't you

see that your muscles – both physical and mental – are becoming stronger with each passing day? You are growing in endurance, fortitude, perseverance and patience. You are learning to face the ridicules of people. Is it a small benefit for you? What more do you want?'

Push your rocks

The same rock attitude applies to our life as well. The rocks of life are the problems we face. Pushing the rocks of life, we become stronger in equanimity, peace, endurance, fortitude and understanding. The problematic situations or rocks will always be there. There will always be difficult people on the way. Their only job would be to cross our lines of progress. There will always be sickness and hospitalization of oneself or of some dear ones. There will always be some birth somewhere and death elsewhere. How can anybody avoid failures and keep winning all the time? How can you make everybody very considerate and remove all negativities from their behavior? These are the inevitables of life. You accept them, good for you. You resist them, bad for you as they will still be there and you will be disturbed too.

When the priorities are pointing outwards, you tend to get bogged down by the difficulties. Or at least, you don't want them there. You just want to reach the goal somehow. There is haste, impatience and unawareness in your behavior. Nature gives difficulties so that your inner obstacles get surfaced and you become aware of them. How else will you understand them and make an effort to remove them?

When the priorities get internalized, i.e., your inner growth becomes paramount for you, your attitude changes completely toward the problems. You are here to *try* to solve them one by one – and to the best of your capabilities. That's it. They get solved, good. They don't get solved, that's also fine. You are not here for finding all the right solutions. Nobody can do that. *For you, the only reality is the Now.* Problems are opportunities of growth for you. You know that you can only do your best with love, awareness and happiness. The rest – only God knows! Solving problems become like solving sums of math.

You also need to understand that all solutions must become new problems eventually. Therefore, you are never in any hurry. Your only goal in life is to do things with peace and awareness – day after day. You just keep on doing your best with a peacefully fulfilled mind and a loving heart.

Fourth law of peace

Completeness = Lack of incompleteness

1. Once a Zen master was asked: 'What is the essence of your teachings?' He said, 'You don't have to do anything. You don't need to go anywhere. You are not required to become anybody.'

2. The 'Life' is filled with happiness up to the brim. The real nature of everybody is happiness. Don't take it as a cliché please. It is clearly experientiable; you just need to follow certain principles. It is like trying to see distant stars with naked eyes. You can't do it because the scope of the eyes is limited. You need to use certain other laws of nature to act as a bridge between your eyes and the stars. A telescope is not a physical instrument. It is the essence of certain laws of nature. It is a certain intelligence in material form.

3. Happiness also needs a bridge. It is like a very near-distant star. There are certain laws of internal nature that act as a bridge that takes you to happiness. The essence of those laws is *'You don't need to desire and chase. Your true nature is happiness'*. It is this desiring only that is acting as a hindrance. Just drop it. Happiness cannot be had if you feel

incomplete due to your X factors. They will always cause incompleteness and thus, unhappiness.

4. *True completeness has only one definition: Lack of incompleteness.*

5. The moment you accept I + X = Completeness, you have already admitted defeat. You are indirectly supporting incompleteness as your current state of being. You are imposing certain distant conditions in order to realize in future what is currently available to you. Your postponement is not only unnecessary, it is also futile.

6. Imagine a state in which you no longer believe that there has to be an X factor for you to be fulfilled. How would you feel then? If you feel bad, you have not understood the whole process. If you feel light and good, then you have understood it right. Now, you just need to practice living in this freedom – freedom from dependence upon X factors.

Fifth law of peace

*Pain is what you get when you step out of your own business
and start interfering in others' business.*

1. The most stressed people in the world are those who are in
    the habit of minding other people's business. They are
    always curious about others. They have a false sense of
    superiority. They think they know the best; but in reality,
    they know the least – even about themselves.

2. There are three kinds of business in this world – my
    business, your business and nature's business. When one
    minds just one's own business, one grows. When one pokes
    one's nose everywhere, one suffers. The beauty of this game
    is that one does not understand that one is suffering. Anger,
    restlessness, pride, stress, worries and jealousy etc. are not
    taken as suffering! These are understood to be life's
    inherent necessities!

3. Those who criticize others are *always* found wanting in the
    same things that they criticize about. Living in glass houses,
    they like throwing stones at others! When others do the
    same, they don't like it!

4. We also need to understand the difference between mindful compassion and impulsive interference. For example, as regards your duty toward your children, your job is to provide the right environment and the best possibilities of growth. Even after having done your best, they may not follow what you think is the best course for them. You will have to draw a line somewhere, lest your own life should get disturbed. Similarly, in other relationships.

5. *Do your best, leave the rest*. While helping others, the odds that one may not get the desired response and one's compassion may get misunderstood are always there. It is important to recognize the difference between interfering and living in compassion. The former disturbs you and the latter gives you pure joy. In the second case, you do your best without imposing any outcome.

Sixth law of peace

You cannot change the past.
You cannot control the future.

Ayala and her family had a strong bond of love with their relations in Israel. They always helped each other. It so happened that Ayala's family had to immigrate to Canada as they got a great business opportunity there. Unfortunately, Ayala's sister passed away within one year of their leaving Israel. When Ayala came to Z Meditation Retreat, it was already four years that she was suffering. She had a strong sense of guilt that it was because of their going to Canada that her sister went into depression and died so soon. She felt that if she had not gone away, her sister would have lived longer.

1. If your intentions are not to harm anybody and something happens just by chance, you are absolutely not responsible. Just pray, bless and help. You should not take it to heart. Loving yourself is also your responsibility.

2. However, if something untoward happens through intent and later on you keep feeling bad about it, that is also not helpful. *Regret and guilt are useful only when you resolve to do it differently the next time.* It is human to make mistakes.

It is normal and natural; but the life does not end there. We need to learn our lessons and move forward.

3. Can we ever undo the past? The past exists only in wavy mental formations – just some memories. The actual happening is already over and it can never be changed. We spoil our perfect present by clinging to the futile wish that the past should have been different.

Hopeless!   Impossible!   Absurd!

4. The same with the future also – just certain wavy mental formations. Another trap of unhappiness! Nobody can control what will happen three minutes from now. Nobody. You can only live up to your best potential in the present. That is your sole obligation. **Just do your best and leave the rest.**

5. *It is not sufficient to have passive awareness of the mental waves of past or future. Unless you root out your habit patterns and false beliefs, you will find it difficult to deal with your mind.* Find out for yourself if your root beliefs are helpful in attaining peace; and if they are true or not. This will give a decisive blow to the restlessness of your mind.

6. When there are worries and insecurities about future, are you more efficient in handling the job at hand? What will be more favorable for a good future – a restless mind or a restful mind? What is more creative in finding solutions to your problems – a restless mind or a restful mind?

7. You are going to give up one day all that you are attached to. Surely! Just think if it is really worth it – trying to change the past or control the future?

8. If you live in past or future, you are also losing the joy of the moment. Is it *prudent* to do so?

Seventh law of peace

What they say about me has nothing to do with who I am. Who can know me better than myself?

David came back home one day and his wife Julia started whining once again. She had seen David and Margaret together in a restaurant and she jumped to various conclusions: "David was in a relationship. David had been lying to her. David did not care for her. She had already sensed that something was wrong a few months before... blah... blah...blah."

It was true that David had gone for lunch with Margaret. They were very good friends, but that was it.

Poor David! He got defensive and tried to pacify his wife. But the more he tried to explain, the worst it became. Julia was not listening at all. Later she decided to leave him for good.

1. What do you think was the best course of action for David? Was he responsible for the suspicion of Julia? Was he at fault anywhere in the whole episode? Was he right in feeling guilt and remorse that Julia left him due to a stupid mistake on his part? Should he not have gone to the restaurant with Margaret?

2. Who knows the truth better – David or Julia? It is such an absurdity that you try to understand yourself using the understanding of others, even if it is wrong! Well, are you responsible for what goes on in the minds of others? Can't you see for yourself who you are? If others are not in a mood to listen to the truth, is it your responsibility?

3. This is the challenge for all of us – *not to take anything personally.* There can be opinion cyclones and maligning storms in the universe; *take it as a part of human nature. When three qualities of the mind function, this is possible.* You need to remain unperturbed and stable.

4. There is another aspect here: they might be right in their opinions. Fine; but *who will do the truth check*? Can anybody else do it for you? If somebody tells you that you are a liar, just do the truth check. Do you lie? If yes, feel grateful to the person that he has helped you become aware. If no, tell him with all your compassion that he is wrong. You don't need to fight. You don't need to be defensive. You don't have to give explanations. It is fine that they think bad about you – it is a rock for you to push and grow in detachment and equanimity.

Remember these laws of peace by heart.

As soon as you get up in the morning,

remind yourself of these laws.

When you go to bed at night,

remind yourself again.

Deep Inquiry

Dig deep. Dig deeper.

1. Mindfulness of restlessness is only a pre-requisite for peace. This just gives you some understanding that your mind is restless. However, it is not a lasting cure. Passive mindfulness can give you relief. But, relief is not cure.

2. Restlessness derives all its food from its roots of desires, incompleteness equations and conditionings – right in that order. Now, we will learn how to detach ourselves from them.

3. The lasting solution to this eternal malady is *right understanding*. You change your perspective. The illusions will drop on their own. It is an effortless and joyful process. Coming to know that all your suffering was based on certain wrong notions and hopeless ideas, you will love to drop them. You will then feel light and free.

4. Deep Inquiry is a systematic process of digging – and digging out – using well-defined questions that you ask yourself. When you get to know the truth through your own rational thinking, the effect is deep. You cannot deny your own

findings; you cannot challenge what you have yourself discovered.

5. It is actually a challenge! When you recognize that you were holding on to certain false ideas, you laugh at yourself and want to give them up. But the next step is tough – really giving them up. You might have cherished them all your life. Not only you, your parents, your teachers, your psychotherapists and the entire society cherishes them! Now you need to flow against the current. They may not understand you. They may think that something is wrong with you. But you need to be indifferent to their sullen beliefs. At the same time, you need to be compassionate also as they don't know the truth and are perhaps not ready for this skill yet.

6. Z Meditation Deep Inquiry is a six-step process of self-questioning that helps you stand aside from your own mind and realize freedom:

a. Standing out of the daydreams and understanding their utilitarian consequences.

b. Digging out the first roots of *causal feelings* and understanding their consequences in terms of the actual *consequential feelings*.

c. Digging out the second roots of *incompleteness equations* and understanding their implications in terms of impermanence and unfulfillment.

d. Digging out the third roots of *general conditionings* and experiencing the effect in terms of happiness and freedom.

e. Understanding the implications of interfering in others' business and finding out what one's own real business is.

f. Reinforcement questioning for making the effect deep and lasting.

7. One needs to be always vigilant lest Deep Inquiry should also become a routine, like any other meditation practice. To obviate that possibility, you should keep these two checks in mind while practicing Deep Inquiry:

a. Do it slowly and mindfully. Don't hasten. You don't have to finish anything. You don't have to go anywhere. If you do the questions well, you will be outgrowing your morbid habit patterns. You will then create a fresh fragrance in your being. What can be more important than the realization of fulfillment within?

b. While asking any question, be aware of its implications. Think deeply about the consequences of the answers that you arrive at. They can be life-altering.

Initial Preparation

Prepare yourself well. The enemy is very strong.

1. When you sit for meditation, your mind must be feeling fresh. Many times, the meditators practice with a tired mind. How is it possible to do that? Some people try to force themselves into getting up early in the morning and do meditation. They experience neither clarity nor upliftment most of the times. I am not saying that it should not be done in the morning. It is just that if you are not a morning person, you will not be able to do it effectively. *It is better late than lethargic.*

2. Mornings have an advantage however. You are not hard pressed by your appointments. You can be regular in your sittings. It can be helpful to start the mornings with light mindful exercises like yoga or studying a scripture that will help you *wake up*. When the mind becomes alert, you can do your meditation.

3. If you think that mornings are just not possible for you, you will have to be very careful in the evenings also. Coming back from work or school, you may be too tired to take up the challenge of deep inquiry. Also, you may be tempted to go somewhere else, i.e., your priorities might be skewed in the evenings. You will need to be very firm with yourself.

4. It is always better to have a short nap in the afternoon or in the evening so that the mind is refreshed for this important task of facing oneself. Please don't listen to those who are against this idea of napping. They may not require it as they don't meditate. Learn to appreciate that your needs can be different. Have clarity about your requirements and serve them as your important obligations.

5. The stomach should be light when you meditate. On a heavy stomach, the mind tends to become lazy.

6. What you do during the rest of the day has a powerful impact on your clarity in meditation. You cannot remain irritated with people around and have a blissful meditation also.

7. Meditation is an outgrowing of your root character-patterns. It is a serious work for realizing peace, happiness and compassion in your heart. It cannot be taken as a routine and monotonous exercise that you must finish somehow. You ought to be looking forward to this most beautiful time of the day.

8. An hour a day, at least. Less than that, you will not come to understand the games your mind plays. What can be more important than this work of honing your own mind?

9. Your friends and company can undo the entire work you do on your meditation seat. Be watchful. Just one comment from somebody can easily bring you back to where you started from. They are all there with so many conditionings alive in their minds. They think that their beliefs are absolutely true. They don't want to change as they apparently derive all their happiness from these very beliefs. It is not your responsibility to shove the truth in somebody's unwilling mind. But it is your responsibility only to remain vigilant so that you can grow and outgrow.

10. Systematic and regular practice is a must. You have to be careful that you don't indulge in spiritual hopping. Find your path and walk on it. All paths are good and can take one to the same goal. You have to see what suits you most. Having decided once, just walk straight on it.

11. While meditating, the back, neck and head must be in a straight line to ensure alertness. Shoulders should be relaxed and lower back pulled up. Sitting on a cushion and keeping the crossed legs on the ground will be helpful for your back. If sitting cross-legged is difficult, sit on a stool without the back support. Be creative in finding the right, comfortable and stable posture for yourself.

This Moment, Mindful Moment.

When else?

There were four thieves living in the city of Kolkata. They decided one day to commit a burglary in a house on the banks of the river Ganges. They came in a boat when everybody was fast asleep. They tied their boat to a tree and entered the house. It took them two hours to carry off everything precious. Coming out with their loot, they put it in the boat and started rowing it. They were all rowing with joy in their hearts as they had become very rich that day. They were all talking about what they would do with all that money.
However, things were to happen differently – as it dawned, they were caught by the police right in front of that house!

In their haste, they had forgotten to untie the boat. They were rowing in vain!

1. You meet many meditators who even after years of practice, say that they cannot still their minds at all. They are as restless as they were when they started years before. You hardly see any change in their behavior also. Why does it happen like that?

2. There are two ways in which you can meditate: you do it for inner growth or you do it mechanically, unaware of the

possibility of change. In the latter case, you do it just because it is a fashion or your teacher has asked you to do it or for any such reason. Following a routine of meditation becomes your daily chore. There is hardly any joy and upliftment in this meditation.

3. It is simple to understand these two different ways. Look at the ladder of evolution and you will appreciate the reasons of these divergent behaviors. If the sensual X factory is big or if there is extreme lethargy, the motivation to do meditation will be missing. If one still does it, one must be doing it for some ulterior purpose and not for outgrowing one's habit patterns.

4. However, if there are not many X factors to hold one back, there is a better possibility that meditation will be deep and joyful.

5. When one becomes aware of the restlessness and suffering and truly wants to get rid of it at any cost, that is when one becomes aware that the boat is tied. Without untying and disentanglement, there is no scope that it will move freely in the waters of bliss and awareness. *Deep Inquiry is like untying this boat and removing the obstacles in the way of realizing one's best potential.*

6. The first step of Z Meditation is like this:

You sit straight and bring your awareness to your breath. With the in-breath, you mentally say 'This Moment'. With the out-breath, you mentally say 'Mindful Moment'. Be aware of the marvel of breathing.

As you are enjoying living in the beauty of the moment, there may arise some disturbing thoughts. When these involuntarily thoughts are there, your awareness will not be there. However, after some time, naturally, you will get your awareness back. You will realize that you had got lost elsewhere.

Now stop. Be aware of the thoughts that disturbed you. Just be aware. The moment you are mindful, these dreams will vanish. Whatever feelings or other mental formations you were experiencing while dreaming, they will all come to rest. It is just the mindfulness of the moment that will remain.

7. Now, do the Deep Inquiry on the dreams that you were lost in. Dig out their roots and be free. You must face yourself and not try to put things under the carpet. This is a very creative, beautiful and efficient way of utilizing one's own thoughts to release the root character-patterns.

The first profound question

"Is it a dream or reality?"

1. As you become aware of your agitation, stop and ask yourself the first profound question which has four implication questions:

I. *Is it a dream or reality?*

   a) Is it relevant in this moment?

   b) Is it useful in this moment?

   c) Is it conducive to peace in this moment?

   d) Am I out of it?

2. There is only one reality – the experience of the moment. The rest, only imaginations.

3. All of us are in contact with one marvel of nature or another in this moment. We can fill this moment with peaceful enjoyment of these marvels, provided the instrument that is being used for experiencing them is tranquil. If the instrument is disturbed, we can neither experience mindfulness nor joy. If the daydreams are there, the

experience of mindfulness, appreciation and enjoyment cannot take place.

4. The answer to the first profound question is 'dream'. Always. If at any point you find yourself saying that it is a 'reality', you haven't understood the question. *You are always asking the question about the mental formations that you were lost in.*

5. Imagine yourself asking the same question when you get out of the night dreams. Can you ever say that you were experiencing reality?

6. There is a hidden implication in the question – "How long will I keep living in these dreams? Isn't it high time that I do something about it? Am I a puppet to my mind? Am I not suffering due to its restlessness? My entire life up to now has been spent in dreaming. Should I not wake up now? For good?"

7. The first implication question means: 'Is it important in this moment? Even if it is something important, can I not wait until I finish meditation and create the space for clear thinking? And if it is really important right now, why am I doing meditation and not trying to reflect on the problem

instead? If it is not important in this moment, why am I dwelling on it?'

8. The second implication question means: 'Does doing circles in one's compulsive imaginations lead to any solution? Is it useful from the most pragmatic and utilitarian standpoint? Does imaginary revolving in the dreams lead to any fruits?'

9. The third implication question means: 'Does restlessness give peace? Happiness? Do I want to be peaceful? What is it that I need to do in order to achieve that?'

10. The fourth implication question means: 'If this question is asked after a night dream, can I ever say *no*? Why? How? What is the inference as regards my state of day dreaming? What can be the consequences if I choose to live in awareness and not in dreams? Will they be good and beneficial for me? What is my criterion for goodness?' 'And if my answer is 'yes', what is stopping me from always living in awareness?'

11. Your world exists in your mind. Your own mind is the *only* direct experience that you always have. You mistakenly identify thoughts for their objects and keep suffering all the time.

12. Detachment from these mental formations – that is a necessary requirement for realizing peace. If it appears to be difficult, we will go deeper and do some more digging.

13. Now practice this first profound question along with the mantra.

Outgrowing the root character-patterns

What appears is just the tip.

1. All of us here in this world want to be fulfilled and complete. Nobody wants to remain unfulfilled. This is a necessary pre-requisite for happiness.

2. Why are people unhappy and restless then? It is due to the imaginary incompleteness and the effort to reach completeness through the fulfillment of desires. If there is incompleteness within, along with the understanding that the fulfillment of certain desires will lead to one's completeness, one will *naturally* desire and have resolves and restlessness related to that.

3. One is mostly undisturbed toward the objects one is indifferent to. It is due to attachment and desires, one gets restless.

4. When one is lost in the restlessness, one is also lost in its roots. In order to be peacefully happy and complete, one needs to wake up from these roots as well. It means that it is not sufficient to be merely aware of the dreams. That is just the first step. Next comes detachment from the deeper levels of dreaming – from one's desires and incompleteness

equations – which form one's deeply ingrained character-patterns. This requires the ability to stand aside and be a witness to one's previous ways of living.

5. Detachment from the root patterns of one's own mind leads to outgrowing them. One can use two thoughtful perspectives to do that:

a. *Utilitarian standpoint*: What are these patterns useful for? Do they help in getting happiness and fulfillment? Was I prepared for the consequences of restlessness and unhappiness when I accepted these roots as a way of my life?

b. *Truth standpoint*: 'Are my beliefs true?' is the most important question for a meditator. *Meditation – blissful residence in eternal pure awareness – cannot be experienced using mechanical means. It requires unwavering adherence to the truth. It also requires persistent detachment from false notions.*

The first root character-pattern: Desires

Desires create restlessness and suffering.

Carly was a participant in one of the meditation retreats held in 2001. She started traveling in India with her girl friend Lisa. But for the last few days before coming to the retreat, they had been living separately.

What had happened was that one day Lisa called her mother in UK. When she came back to the room of the guest-house where she was living with Carly, she started screaming at Carly and insulted her for no apparent reason! She dug out many forgotten stories and called names.

In the retreat, Carly was naturally disturbed by Lisa's behavior. The scenes of that day kept flashing. The good times they had spent together, the love that they had for each other and the way it broke for no reason – she was having these involuntary dreams all the time.

1. She wanted to be peaceful and learn how to meditate. As she did the first question of the deep inquiry, she got some space. She understood that her restlessness was just a mental formation and she was attached with it. While attached, she was lost in it and was considering it to be

something very real. Becoming aware, she realized how useless it was to remain lost. It did not fulfill the related desire and it also did not give her peace. In replying to the fourth sub-question, her first response was 'no'! She was not able to detach, despite the understanding that she was trying to detach from a dream only.

2. Why was it difficult for Carly to come out of the daydream? She was attached with the roots of agitation and she was unaware of it. The first root was her *desires*. Carly understood that in order to fully come out of dreams, it is necessary to let go of the desires. Otherwise, it is not possible at all.

3. Now, she needed to contemplate through the second deep inquiry question and understand her feelings. In this process of understanding, detachment and letting go happens on its own.

The second profound question

"What are the feelings hidden in the dream?"

1. If you say that you are out of the dream and you have clearly understood that detachment from your mental waves constitutes freedom, you have won the first battle. Still, there is a distinct possibility of forgetfulness and getting clouded by your previous patterns. If, on the other hand, you have not come out of the dream and the understanding is hazy, you need the furtherance of the deep inquiry all the more.

2. The second profound question also has four implication questions:

II.   *What are the feelings hidden in the dream?*

a)   What are the *causal feelings*? (State all the sets in the form of 'I like that...' and 'I dislike that...' etc.)

b)   What are the *consequential feelings*?

c)   Do I want to be peaceful?

d)   Keeping the causal feelings alive, can I attain peace?

3. This profound question is meant to understand why we get restless. It makes is see if we have happy feelings or unhappy ones. Normally, when you are lost in dreams, there is total involvement in the feelings also. You become the feelings, in a way. In that situation, it is not possible to understand and work on the mind – one is too lost there.

4. *The causal feelings are in the form of these pairs of opposites: liking and disliking; desire and aversion; love and hate; hope and hopelessness; expectation and callousness etc.* For the sake of simplicity, we will mostly work with *liking and disliking*.

5. There can be more than one set of causal feelings in your mind. Each dream can be loaded with a complex of desires.

6. It is necessary to stand aside and be aware. When you do that, you are out of the feelings. You experience awareness and understanding. You are no longer getting buffeted about.

7. The restlessness of your mind is never due to people and things. It is rather due to your desires and expectations from them that cause all the suffering and turmoil. When there is indifference, it does not cause any flutter in your mind.

8. The consequential feelings are wide-ranging: sadness, anger, depression, dejection, feeling low, burden, boredom, irritation, hatred, frustration, disappointment, weakness, fear, worry, rejection, stress, inferiority etc. on the one hand and excitement, pleasure, feeling high etc. on the other.

9. Is it difficult to understand that if you want to get rid of your restlessness and suffering, you have to let go their causes – the causal feelings? Keeping your desires and aversions alive, you cannot be peaceful! Now we reach a very important point in the deep inquiry: *prioritization*. What do you really want: the outside or the inside? You can of course choose the former, but you will have to be ready to accept the consequences as well. Desires will always lead to agitation, frustration, anger and other unhappy feelings. Do you *really* want that?

10. Think deeply. What is it that you are giving up in order to be peaceful? You are not running away to a forest or joining a monastery. You are where you are and you will be where you will be. It is just that you can now have more space if you detach from the causal feelings. You are appreciating and accepting that certain mental formations always give birth to agitation, which you don't want in yourself. You now intelligently decide, without any compulsion, that for you,

peace, happiness and awareness are more important than expecting and hating. You renounce the illusion that desiring will lead to happiness – as it never does.

11. Think more deeply. *What you have decided to detach yourself from is also a dream*; albeit at a deeper subconscious level. Your desires and aversions were also your mental formations. You were just deeply attached and lost in them. You have in reality given up nothing but dreaming!

12. Can Carly be peaceful without dropping her desires? Can desiring be separated from sadness, irritation and anger?

The second root character-pattern:
Incompleteness Equations

Does fulfillment of desires lead to fulfillment?

1. Carly cannot attain peace of mind if her desire that 'Lisa should not have insulted her' remains alive. She sometimes feels angry, sometimes sad and sometimes helpless and the cause of all this is this desire that it should not have happened.

2. Now, she wants to attain peace at any cost. She does not want to harbor the bitter feelings anymore. She understands that she cannot undo the past. Therefore, she has to give up this desire.

3. In reality, the price of peace is no price at all. It just requires letting go of the imaginary and false connection between desires and happiness. This understanding needs to be earnest and clear. Carly's inquiry went on like this:

I.	*Is it a dream or reality?*	**Dream. Only my mental formations.**
a)	Is it relevant in this moment?	**No. Not at all.**
b)	Is it useful in this moment?	**No. No way.**

c) Is it conducive to peace?　　**No. It is just the opposite.**

d) Am I out of it?　　**No. I want to, but it is difficult.**

II.　*What are the feelings hidden in the dream?*

a) What are the *causal feelings*? (State all the sets in the form of 'I like that...' and 'I dislike that...')

I like that Lisa should not have insulted me.
I dislike that she did.

I like that Lisa should have apologized.
I dislike that she did not.

I like that our friendship should not have broken.
I dislike that it did.

b) What are the *consequential feelings*?

I am sad; sometimes angry; sometimes helpless. I cannot meditate and enjoy the moment.

c) Do I want to be peaceful?

Yes. Nothing else is more important for me.

d) Keeping the causal feelings alive, can I attain peace?

No. I truly want to give up my hopeless desires.

4. Carly understood that these two feelings could not remain together in the mind: desiring and peace. She decided to let go her desires – her likings and dislikings. This was a big

character shift in her life. She had made her first fruitful attempts at growing spiritually. When she finally made up her mind – and it was only a question of making up the mind – she felt *'so much relief'*.

5. Now we want to go to the roots of desiring. Why do we have desires? Why do we like certain things and dislike others? If it causes us pain, why do we do that?

6. The simple answer is: *We do that because we want to be complete and happy. The equation 'I + X = C' is at the root of desiring.* We have been unconsciously tutored by our society that we can attain completeness and happiness *only* when our desires get fulfilled. Actually, people in our world are so attached to this way of thinking that they have lost the ability to do the reality check. *We are all following each other in this blind alley of ignorance.* We do not learn from the mistakes of others – nay, we do not learn even from our own mistakes.

7. This means that restlessness is due to desires and desires are due to our deep-seated want to be complete and happy. 'I + X = C' is the second deeply embedded root. On reflection, Carly realized that the fulfillment of desires does not lead to lasting fulfillment. She does get some temporary

pleasure, but it does not last. 'Desiring' continues to remain, as *the values do not change when desires get fulfilled.* In reality, we are unwittingly creating more misery and turmoil in our lives by believing in the illusion of incompleteness.

8. The next profound question in the Deep Inquiry is asked in order to remove the illusion of incompleteness. We ask about the Í + X = C' equations and their consequences. As a result, we get detached from these equations also and clear our way to freedom.

The third profound question

"What are the incompleteness equations hidden in the dream?"

State all the equations in the form of 'I + X = C' and then ask yourself:

>   a. If these desires get fulfilled, will I get lasting peace?

>   b. What is my own history?

>   c. Am I attaching myself with something permanent?

>   d. Can incompleteness ever give completeness and freedom?

1. In answering the main question, fill up your X factors in the equation 'I + X = C'. You must come out with as many equations as you have. Each dream thought might be loaded with several equations that you are normally unaware of. These sets will be related to your answers to the second profound question.

2. You have already understood that you just have an illusion of incompleteness. You have X factors because you believe that they will give you fulfillment and happiness. In reality,

they only cause dissatisfaction. Incompleteness can be removed only by letting go of all the X factors.

3. The first implication question makes you understand that even when your desires get fulfilled, you still remain unfulfilled as you have other X factors in your life and you are prone to having more in the days to come. You can never get *lasting peace or happiness* by the fulfillment of desires. However, some temporary spurts of excitement do take place. They make you forget your dissatisfaction for some time. But soon afterwards, you come back to the same old state of incompleteness.

4. Your own life history always tells you that in spite of the fulfillment of so many of your desires, you are still unfulfilled. The proof of unfulfillment is that you still have all these incompleteness equations alive in you. Your life consists of continuous shifting from one X factor to another.

5. These two implication questions take us to an infallible inference: *This is not the way.* Keeping the old perspective intact, it is not possible to experience lasting peace and happiness. It is not by keeping the X factors, but by burning the X factory itself that you can get this sublime state of freedom.

6. The objects of desires are impermanent. The desires themselves are impermanent. The related feelings are impermanent. What is it that we are attaching ourselves with?

7. Completeness has only one definition: **CESSATION OF INCOMPLETENESS**. The illusion that there must be dependence in order to become happy is the root cause of suffering. Unless you drop it and accept the state of completeness, unconditioned and without any dependence whatsoever, there is no hope. You will never be able to reach eternal joy and freedom using the desire route.

8. How did Carly proceed further toward freedom?

III. *What are the incompleteness equations hidden in the dream?* (State all the equations in the form of 'I + X = C' or I + Y = IC or I − X = C or I − Y = IC, whichever is most appropriate)

    i.   **I + Lisa should not have insulted me = Completeness**
           I + Lisa insulted me = Incompleteness

    ii.   **I + Lisa should have apologized = Completeness**
           I + Lisa did not apologize = Incompleteness

    iii.   **I + Our friendship should not have broken =**

Completeness

I + Our friendship broke = Incompleteness

a) If these desires get fulfilled, will I get lasting peace?

   No. I don't think so. When we were friends, I was not peaceful for certain other reasons. Even if Lisa apologizes, I don't think that that in itself is a sufficient reason for me to get lasting peace. However, I will feel good for some time if she does that.

b) What is my own history?

   I keep falling into similar traps of unhappiness every now and then. This is not the first time in my life that a friend has insulted me and our friendship broke in this manner. Initially, it hurts. But I continue living my life and after some time I forget.

c) Am I attaching myself with something permanent?

   Nothing is permanent in this world. Not even friendships; nor the feelings.

d) Can incompleteness ever give completeness and freedom?

   Never. I want to achieve inner completeness. I want to drop all my X factors!

9. We understand that closing the X-factor accounts one by one by the fulfillment of related desires is not the way to lasting peace and freedom. We now recognize that the only way is by burning the X factory altogether. It means we choose not to have any dependence whatsoever in our lives.

10. At this juncture, there are some important questions that you may ask yourself:

a. Do you want to proceed further?

b. If yes, what is the cause of incompleteness equations?

c. If no, why?

Common Conditionings

Conditionings are just relative ideas.

1. Why is it that in some countries, they abhor the idea of *living together* before marriage and in some others, it is a common way of life? Why is it that they hate people eating beef at one place and at another, it is normal to do so? Why do people have divergent cultures?

2. Now we need to understand the general beliefs of societies. All over the world, there are certain *universal programs or conditionings* and there are some *local ones*. When a child is born, it is fed with these conditionings from day one. They might not be doing it purposely, but living in a conditioned environment, it happens automatically. As most of us live in unawareness, we cannot understand that we are getting conditioned. We sincerely feel that our beliefs are absolute truths and there should never be a mis-match of the beliefs with the reality. Whenever a mis-match takes place, pain is the result.

3. The conditionings are stated in an impersonal way. Some examples of *universal conditionings* are:

a. Money gives happiness.

b. People should always love others.

c. Good friendship should never end.

d. There should never be divorce.

e. Love should be reciprocated.

f. One should not get insulted in public.

g. One's good work should get acknowledged.

h. Status and power give fulfillment.

i. One's love-life should be respected by others.

j. People should not interfere in others' business.

k. Spiritual teachers should live what they say.

l. Children should respect their parents.

m. Parents should always be there for their children.

n. Parents should give space to their children.

o. There should not be betrayal in friendship.

p. There should not be adultery by one's partner.

q. Both parents should always bring up the children together.

r. Bosses should not scream.

s. Workers in a company should work hard and smart.

t. Good teams should always win.

u. Everybody should respect everybody else.

v. People should not steal.

w. There should not be war.

x. Environment should be respected.

y. Politicians should not be crooked.

z. Media should be responsible.

aa. There should not be problems in life.

bb. One should not fall sick / be sent to hospital.

cc. There should be balance in all spheres of life.

dd. Truth should always prevail.

ee. Wives should be obedient and loving.

ff. Husbands should listen to and take care of their wives.

gg. True love should always last.

hh. One should not be disturbed in one's sleep.

ii. Beds should be comfortable.

jj. Privacy of people should be respected.

kk. Bus rides should never be bumpy.

ll. People should not ask unnecessary questions.

   lm. Students in meditation retreats should be quick in learning.

   ln. People should not be obese.

   Etc.

4. *Some local conditionings* are:

 a. Meat eating is bad.

 b. One should not eat beef.

 c. One should not eat pigs.

 d. Children should not live with their parents when they become adults.

 e. Children should always live with their parents.

 f. Before marriage, lovers should not live together.

 g. Before marriage, lovers should live together.

 h. People should work hard for money.

i. People should not give their lives for money.

j. One should not keep the knife standing in butter.

k. One's cap should not be put on the ground.

l. A cat should not cross one's path.

5. These are the definitions of right-wrong, good-bad, auspicious-inauspicious etc. of groups of people like countries, tribes and communities. For example, a group of people can believe that 'there should not be *living together* before marriage as it is a corrupt practice.' This general belief of the group is its conditioning or a program that it unconsciously assumes to be an absolute truth. Generally, people don't understand the difference between an absolute truth and a relative truth. The latter can just be need based. Considering the relative as absolute, people frown, scorn, jeer, get upset, get depressed, commit suicides and even commit crimes!

6. Desires and incompleteness equations get sculpted according to the conditionings. When one believes in 'there should not be *living together* before marriage as it is a corrupt practice', one will naturally have a desire that one's near and dear ones should not go against this norm. If

somebody breaks this rule, one gets angry or upset depending on the gravity of the belief in the conditioning and the type of relationship.

7. All conditionings are just some notions that people take to be true. The societies create them for their smooth running. But they pay a big price in the form of misery of its people. As the mind consists of three qualities and not just one, there will always be big gaps between the beliefs and the reality. People cannot always walk straight. It is impossible. But we are not ready to accept that, especially in the cases of our near and dear ones. Hence we suffer.

8. Most of the people living in the world belong to lethargy and sensuality. In their minds, there is strong attachment with the conditionings and there is hardly any possibility of detachment. The spiritual science is an objective science as it is based on certain solid principles and the truths can be verified by anybody. However, it is subjective also as one has to deserve entering this lab. If one is always living in the mind and has no inclination to detach, i.e., if one really feels that one's beliefs are absolutely true, why will one try to come out of them? One will have zero motivation to do that. Peace is not a priority for most people here. And why should it be?! If you want to be free, the solution is that you

yourself follow these norms for the sake of peace in yourself and in the society. But if others are not following, try to understand them with a loving heart. The state of being free from all conditionings can happen to an individual, and not to a group of people. If somebody achieves that, there will be perfect harmony with the flow of events. There will be unconditioned peace in the mind and loving understanding in the heart. This is freedom.

The fourth profound question

"What are the general conditionings hidden in the dream?"

1. Why do you have incompleteness equations? What made you believe in them? In order to reach the roots of incompleteness equations, let us now take up the fourth profound question, which has five implication questions:

IV. *What are the general conditionings hidden in the dream?* (State all the conditionings and do the work on each one separately.)

a. Is it reality?

b. What is the reality?

c. How do I feel when I am attached with this wrong notion?

d. How do I feel if I detach from this wrong notion?

e. What is preventing me from giving up this painful story?

2. 'That people should always be respectful to each other' leads to 'I + My friend should respect me = Completeness / Happiness'. This desire for happiness leads to 'I want that my friend should not disrespect me' and 'I want that my friend should always respect me.' Now all these statements

in the quotes are dreams. One has them in the background of the mind. As soon as something contrary happens in your life, you suffer. If something favorable happens, you feel good. But it also makes you expect – which means that you can be restless, edgy and scared that something adverse may happen in the future.

3. There are two types of conditionings:

a. *Should* conditionings – These are of the following forms: 'people *should* be compassionate', 'love *should* be reciprocated', 'there *should* not be problems in life' etc.

b. *Unhappiness* conditionings – 'money gives happiness', 'attachment to children gives happiness', 'fulfillment of desires gives happiness' etc. That is, 'happiness comes from some external source'.

4. Both these types always give unhappiness as they are absolutely not true – they don't *always* correspond to the reality. The reality *can* be different and that is what causes suffering. If you are not adaptable to the reality of the world, you will live in pain. This pain can be there in the form of any of the consequential feelings. You might even have a very compassionate heart – but that is not sufficient for peace and fulfillment.

5. Attaching with conditionings is pain. Detachment is freedom.

6. If you understand that these are just certain false romantic ideas, and if you are a sane person, why will you not give them up? It is just these absurd mental formations that stop you from realizing your best potential! What does it cost to give them up?

7. The only person who can prevent you from detaching from a painful story is you. Do you still want to live in pain? Don't you see that your old ideas are stale and agonizing? Do you want to wake up now? Can you do it now?

8. When I first understood the deep inquiry, it was like the biggest revolution of my life. I was smiling at my age-old stupidities. How funny one can be!

9. Carly proceeded further:

IV. *What are the general conditionings hidden in the dream?* (State all the conditionings and do the work on each one separately.)

Friends should respect each other
Friends should not insult each other; especially for no reason whatsoever.

Good friendship should remain.

Good friendship should not have an abrupt and bad end.

If a friend makes a mistake, she should apologize.

Friends should not be callous towards each others' feelings.

Friendship gives happiness.

a. Is it reality?

No.

b. What is the reality?

Friends do insult their friends.

Good friendships do break.

Friends are callous sometimes.

Friendship causes pain also.

c. How do I feel when I am attached with these wrong notions?

Sad; sometimes angry; cannot enjoy the moment; cannot meditate.

d. How do I feel if I detach from this wrong notion?

I feel that a big load has been lifted off my head.

I feel light.

I can now understand Lisa.

I am in the moment now and wondering how a wrong notion can cause so many problems in one's mind.

I feel the flow of acceptance in my heart. It is soothing.

I feel free now. I understand that my happiness comes only from me.

e. What is preventing me from giving up this painful story?

Only I can stop me. I will not let that happen.

I want to accept. I don't want to resist the reality anymore and suffer.

10. Just see how damaging can be our stories! And how liberating is giving them up! What is holding us back is our own mind. We need to detach from it in order to experience freedom. This is the sweetest possible living on the planet. The next story is very relevant.

The Mirror

It's the way you face life that makes the difference.

One day when all the employees reached the office, they saw a big note on the door on which it was written: "Yesterday the person who has been hindering your growth in this company passed away. We invite you to join the funeral in the room that has been prepared in the Gym." They all felt sad for the death of one of their colleagues, but after a while they got curious to know who this colleague was? The excitement in the gym was such that the security agents were ordered to control the crowd within the room. Each of them wondered: 'Who is this guy who was hindering my progress? Well, at least he died!' One by one, as the curious employees got closer to the coffin, and when they looked inside it, each of them become speechless. They stood near the coffin, shocked and in silence, as if someone had touched the deepest part of their soul. There was a mirror inside the coffin: everyone who looked inside it could see himself. There was also a sign next to the mirror that said: 'There is only one person who is capable to set limits to your growth: It is YOU.'

You are the only person who can revolutionize your life. You are the only person who can influence your happiness and your success. You are the only person who can help yourself. Your life does not change when your boss changes, when your friends change, when your parents change, when your partner changes, when your company changes. Your life changes when you change, when you go beyond your limiting beliefs, when you realize that you are the only one responsible for your life. The most important relationship you can have is the one you have with yourself. Examine yourself, watch yourself. Don't be afraid of difficulties, impossibilities and losses. Be a winner: build yourself and your reality. It's the way you face life that makes the difference.

The fifth profound question

"Whose business?"

1. The fifth law of peace is 'Pain is what you get when you step out of your own business.' If you interfere in others' business and try to control them, you will suffer. But most of us feel that people, especially our relations, should be under our control. They say how can you accept your husband do whatever he likes; how can you accept your wife flirting with others; how can you accept your children coming late from parties every day...... Is it not one's moral duty to try to interfere and bring people on the right path? Is it not our ethical responsibility to criticize for the sake of smooth running of the relationships and society?

2. I will like to repeat what I have written before:

a. Those who criticize are *always* found wanting in the same things that they criticize others about. Living in glass houses, they like throwing stones at others! When others do the same, they don't like it!

b. We also need to understand the difference between mindful compassion and impulsive interference. For example, as regards your duty toward your children, your job is to provide the right environment and the best possibilities of growth. Of course, it is your dharma to give them the right guidance. But, the point is that even after having done your best, they may not follow what you think is the best course for them. *You will have to draw a line somewhere, lest your own life should get disturbed*. Similarly, in other relationships. If your husband has decided to shift his commitment to somebody else, why do you still want to run after him? Bless him that he may find true fulfillment. Can you change his mind by using force or by getting angry? Don't you want to see him happy? His thinking may not be conducive to realizing true happiness, but is yours conducive? Is he amenable to listening? You have to create such an inner environment that you remain balanced in all situations. Those who are going away, bless them. Those who are coming to you, help them. If you can do it, you will be a free person.

c. *Do your best, leave the rest*. While helping others, the odds that you may not get the desired response and your compassion may get misunderstood are always there. It is important to recognize the difference between interfering and living in compassion and peace. The former disturbs you and the latter gives you pure joy. In the second case, *you do your best without imposing any outcome.*

3. Both the *should* and *unhappiness* conditionings can to be profited from. They are beneficial because they help us understand our business better. The fifth profound question has two implication questions:

V. *Whose business?*

a. Am I stepping out of my own business and interfering?

b. What is my real business in this moment?

4. As you reflect and analyze further, you will undoubtedly realize that you were interfering in somebody else's business. What goes on in others' minds and how they behave is not your business, nor responsibility. *Nobody will change just because you want them to change. They will change only when they themselves will want to.* They have their own deep grooves of personality based on the three qualities of the mind and their X factors. *They sincerely feel that their path is the best path for them.* Who are you to say that they are wrong?

5. Will it not be a disservice if we shatter the faith of a person? We must see whether he deserves what we want to offer. If

not, why offer? If yes, is he asking us? If yes, are we doing it with peace and compassion or with an impulsive desire that he should listen to us? Everybody is acting compulsively, in a way. We have to be aware that we don't do that in the name of love!

Turn-in

1. Your only obligation is you. Just you. For answering the second implication question of the fifth one, do a self analysis. Just **turn-in** the *should* conditionings upon yourself and see if you are yourself living up to what you expect of others. For example, if your conditioning was 'people should respect each other', your turn-ins can be of two kinds:

a. *Me-first* turn-ins: You can be very creative in inferring these:

   'I should respect myself.'

   'I should respect people.'

   'I should respect the person from whom I am expecting respect.'

   When you are doing the turn-ins, also ask yourself, "Am I doing it?" These turn-ins make you realize that you have to first live it yourself. That is your only business and sole obligation. Not expecting anything from others and concentrating just on your own business shown by the turn-ins will immediately lead to *unconditioned peace*. You will feel good when you understand what you are lacking in and what your real business is. *You are no longer looking for scapegoats for your unhappiness.* You don't want to waste your energy in blaming and expecting. Rather, you now concentrate on your real responsibility of unconditioned peace and fulfillment.

b. *Acceptance* turn-ins:

'I accept that people can be disrespectful.'
'I accept that my friend can be unaware.'

This naturally leads to the understanding that nobody is to be blamed as there is an unconscious compulsion of personality that is built-in by nature and not by any humans. One will now be more aware and experience *unconditioned loving kindness*.

7. *Unconditioned peace and love are your primary obligations – foremost dharma.* If this is achieved, the rest will easily fall in place. Your mind will be so much at ease and your heart will be so much full of kindness that you will not find anything difficult or problematic. You will start living your life moment by moment, day by day – full of peace and love. What more do you want? You are already there on the highest peak. Now, you just have to maintain yourself there.

8. Afterwards, if you find yourself forgetting and getting restless due to any reason, you will need to do the deep inquiry again. Each time you get lost, you will need to wake

up again… and again... and again. Gradually, you will see that living on the highest peak will no longer remain a difficult job. You will, with consistent practice, create new grooves of understanding. Living in this freedom perspective will become a natural habit.

9. As regards the unhappiness conditionings that are similar to the illusion of incompleteness, the turn-ins are very simple. For 'Friendship gives happiness', the turn-in are:

'I give myself happiness.'
'Friendship may not give happiness.

These turn-ins are meant to remind us that there is only one possibility of arriving at a state of freedom and completeness: cessation of incompleteness. That is, independence from all X factors. There is no other way.

The last profound question

"Why should I give up my real business ever?"

1. Let it be a thoughtful and conscious decision:

VI.   *Why should I give up my real business ever?*

2. Once you are aware that your conditionings, incompleteness equations and desires are harmful for you, why would you like to get trapped by them again? Unless you want it, they cannot get attached with you. You have to decide what kind of life you want to live – now onwards. It can be peaceful, blissful and loveful, or it can be painful. You will need to make a clear and decisive choice.

3. This choice is about *your life in totality*. What you practice and understand on your meditation seat will need to be practiced in the real life also. The differentiation between spiritual and secular ought not to remain for a sincere aspirant of freedom.

4. It is not that doing the deep inquiry once, you will be free from your conditionings forever. That is an ideal case. Most of us here are not ideal cases. The momentum of our past habit- patterns can cause restlessness again and we will

have to patiently and systematically crush it again. It requires a life-long commitment. It needs agile awareness all the time. Slowly and slowly, as you go on practicing, the new right-understanding patterns will become strong.

5. You will need to have patience and keep practicing with serenity. There is no short-cut to freedom. And the rewards are priceless – you know that!

Six profound questions

I. *Is it a dream or reality?*

a) Is it relevant in this moment?

b) Is it useful in this moment?

c) Is it conducive to peace in this moment?

d) Am I out of it?

II. *What are the feelings hidden in the dream?*

a) What are the causal feelings?

b) What are the consequential feelings?

c) Do I want to be peaceful?

d) Keeping the causal feelings alive, can I attain peace?

III. What *are the incompleteness equations hidden in the dream?*

a) If these desires get fulfilled, will I get lasting peace?

b) What is my own history?

c) Am I attaching myself with something permanent?

d) Can incompleteness ever give completeness and freedom?

IV. *What are the general conditionings hidden in the dream?*

a) Is this reality?

b) What is the reality?

c) How do I feel when I am attached with a wrong notion?

d) How do I feel if I am detached from the wrong notion?

e) What is preventing me from give up a painful story?

V. *Whose business?*

a) Am I stepping out of my business and interfering?

b) What is my real business in this moment?

VI. Why should I give up my real business ever?

Some case studies

John Mayor

Let us take a hypothetical situation for John. Imagine that it was not a dream and it happened in reality. How would John do the deep inquiry if it had happened in reality? Let us suppose that John is meditating on 'This Moment. Mindful Moment.' An agitation arises in his mind about his wife's strange behavior. As he wakes up, his deep inquiry could be like this:

I. *Is it a dream or reality?*

    I was experiencing my own thoughts and I was lost in it. It was a dream.

a) Is it relevant in this moment?

    Only living in the moment is relevant.

b) Is it useful in this moment?

    No. Just a futile dream. My wife will not change just because I want her to.

c) Is it conducive to peace in this moment?

    No. I am disturbed.

d) Am I out of it?

    Not really. I wish she did not behave like that.

II.	*What are the feelings hidden in the dream?*

a)	What are the causal feelings?

I like that Nancy trusts me.

I like that Nancy does not behave so stupidly.

I want her to be happy and peaceful.

I like to have a peaceful relationship with Nancy.

I dislike what she does and thinks, as it is all non-sense.

b)	What are the consequential feelings?

I get angry.

I feel like running away from her.

I start disliking her and my love for her gets replaced by hatred.
I am unhappy and sad.
I cannot meditate.

c)	Do I want to be peaceful?

Yes.

d)	Keeping the causal feelings alive, can I attain peace?

No. I need to weigh things clearly.

III.	*What are the incompleteness equations hidden in the dream?*

I + sane Nancy = completeness and happiness

I + suspicious Nancy = incompleteness and unhappiness

a) If these desires get fulfilled, will I get lasting peace?

I don't think so. This is just one of the several accounts in my life. If this desire gets fulfilled, I have so many other issues hanging. When I had a good relationship with her, even then I was restless.

b) What is my own history?

Even when my desires get fulfilled, I remain unfulfilled as there is always something else.

c) Am I attaching myself with something permanent?

No. Nothing remains. The past situations have not remained. This one will also pass away.

d) Can incompleteness ever give completeness and freedom?

Never. I only want inner completeness. Nothing less than that, whatever the cost.

IV. *What are the general conditionings hidden in the dream?*

Wives should not be suspicious.

Wives should not misunderstand husbands.

a) Is this reality?

No.

b) What is the reality?

Wives do misunderstand husbands. Wives can be suspicious.

c) How do I feel when I am attached with these wrong notions?

Angry, sad, I hate Nancy...

I do not want to feel like that. I want to be happy. I love her.

d) How do I feel if I detach from this wrong notion?

I can understand her attachment and possessiveness. I am more aware. I feel balanced and light.

e) What is preventing me from give up these painful stories?

Nothing. I have given them up.

V. *Whose business?*

a) Am I stepping out of my business and interfering?

How Nancy feels is her business. If I interfere, I suffer. I don't want to suffer anymore.

b) What is my real business in this moment?

Me. Only me. I should understand my needs.

I should be considerate to myself.

I should understand Nancy's needs.

I should understand human needs.

I should understand the needs of people around me.

I accept that wives may not understand husbands. There can be misunderstanding due to possessiveness.

I accept it and I accept her as she is.

VI. *Why should I give up my real business ever?*

No reason. I don't want to be sad and angry again.

Susan Claire

Susan was unhappy with her job. It was a big burden for her to go to the office everyday as she thought that her real passion was teaching kids. When she came to Z Meditation Centre to do the retreat, her whole being looked exhausted due to the work pressure.

She wanted to go back to her country with a clear mind. When Susan was doing meditation in order to understand and experience the bliss of the moment, these thoughts about her desire to change the job came and disturbed her again. Then she did the deep inquiry.

I.   *Is it a dream or reality?*
     A dream. I am in India; I am not in the office now.

   a) Is it relevant in this moment?
      No. And yes also as I want to resolve it now.

   b) Is it useful in this moment?
      No. And yes. I want a solution.

   c) Is it conducive to peace in this moment?
      No. I am tired.

   d) Am I out of it?

      No. I want to resolve it once for all.

II.   *What are the feelings hidden in the dream?*

a)   What are the causal feelings?

I like that I have passion for what I do.

I dislike the routine office work.

I want to live for kids. I love teaching.

I don't want to go back to the office again.

b)   What are the consequential feelings?

I am tired.

I feel like a misfit in my office.

I am also scared about my financial security if I leave my job.

I am not able to enjoy this moment and what I have.

c)   Do I want to be peaceful?

Yes. I want to be happy.

d)   Keeping the causal feelings alive, can I attain peace?

No.

III.   *What are the incompleteness equations hidden in the dream?*

I + teaching kids = completeness and satisfaction

I + going to office = incompleteness

I + less pressure at work = happiness

I + deadlines = unhappiness

a) If these desires get fulfilled, will I get lasting peace?

When I think about it, I realize that it has been a strong pattern in my life. Wherever I am, I am dissatisfied. Before I got the current job two years ago, I was unhappy and I desperately wanted to get this job. Now I am unhappy again.

b) What is my own history?

Same patterns keep repeating.

c) Am I attaching myself with something permanent?

No. The past had something else. The future will have something else.

d) Can incompleteness ever give completeness and freedom?

No. I understand that I will need to let go my X factor; only then I can be complete. I realize that it has also to do with all the troubles at the office. If it were an easy job, I won't mind it so much.

Secondly, the salary is also not according to the work that I do.

My company should be considerate.

It is actually a very complex situation.

IV. *What are the general conditionings hidden in the dream?*

All of one's desires should get fulfilled.

There should not be any problems in life.

There should be financial security.

The pay should be according to the work (pressure).

The employers should be considerate to the employees.

One should be able to do what one likes.

a) Is this reality?

No.

b) What is the reality?

These are just hopeless notions. The reality is just the opposite. My life is my greatest teacher of reality.

c) How do I feel when I am attached with these stories?

Exhausted. I just want to relax all the time. I don't like anything. I am tired all the time.

d) How do I feel if I detach from this wrong notion?

I feel that I am standing aside and looking at my hopeless stories with detachment. I am mindful now. I have composure. I think I can confront my life with much more ease and balance.

e) What is preventing me from give up these painful stories?

Only I can prevent myself. I don't want to do it anymore. But I also understand that there is a lot of work ahead.

V. *Whose business?*

a) Am I stepping out of my business and interfering?

I think it is my business in one way. But how things happen in life is not my business. My business is what I do with what happens in life.

b) What is my real business in this moment?

To live in the moment and enjoy it. The office problems and even the life's problems can never be solved for good.

Something will always remain unsolved.

Some desires will not get fulfilled. Some will. This is the way. I accept it as it is.

I am prepared to face my problems.

I do think that I will like teaching kids more as that appears to be my dharma. But that is not important in this moment. I will need to take a thoughtful decision in this regard and I will do it when I go back. Right now, it is just this mindful moment!

VI. *Why should I give up my real business ever?*

I want to live my life in awareness. There is no reason that I give up my freedom now.

Note: We need to differentiate between daydream agitations and conscious intelligent thinking. Walking on one's dharma ought to be a priority, no doubt. But just doing circles around this thought and remaining stressed about it is not good.

First attain peace by freeing yourself of conditionings. Then take your decisions wisely and prudently.

Did you notice how there is a shift from 'passion for job' and teaching kids' to 'financial security', 'pressure-free work' and 'insufficient salary'. When you do the Inquiry, you are able to dig out your real attachments and fixations. Many times, they remain hidden behind a veil of pseudo dharma.

Enat

Enat was disturbed that her mother was not well. Her mother was feeling very lonely in Israel. Enat was in France and had to write her exam the next day. She loved her mother and wanted to be with her ASAP. Therefore, she was not able to concentrate on her studies...

I. *Is it a dream or reality?*

A dream. My mind is over-active now. I am not able to control it.

   a) Is it relevant in this moment?

No. I have my main exam tomorrow. It is important for me that I study.

   b) Is it useful in this moment?

No. I can't go there now and I cannot concentrate also.

   c) Is it conducive to peace in this moment?

No.

   d) Am I out of it?

No. I love my mother. I can't see her suffering.

II. *What are the feelings hidden in the dream?*

   a) What are the causal feelings?

I like to be with my mother when she needs me.

I dislike that she suffers and feels lonely.

I want her to be strong.

b) What are the consequential feelings?

I feel helpless and sad.

I also feel lonely.

c) Do I want to be peaceful?

Yes.

d) Keeping the causal feelings alive, can I attain peace?

No.

Does it mean that I detach myself from my mother? It is difficult.

III. *What are the incompleteness equations hidden in the dream?*

I + being with my mother = completeness

I - being with my mother = incompleteness

I + my mother consoled = completeness

I - my mother consoled = completeness

a) If this desire gets fulfilled, will I get lasting peace?

It will be a big relief for me, but it will not give lasting peace, for sure. I know that even when I am with my mother, she has some reason or the other to remain unhappy. I have never been able to fulfill all her wants.

b) What is my own history?

I am vulnerable to attracting unhappiness of others. Not only my mother, when my friends are unhappy, I also become unhappy.

c) Am I attaching myself with something permanent?

No. Life's situations and problems keep changing. I know that if I don't go back to Israel now and explain my situation to her, she can be quite amenable. She will understand and accept.

d) Can incompleteness ever give completeness and freedom?

No. Never. I want to be strong and complete within myself.

IV. *What are the general conditionings hidden in the dream?*

Mothers should not miss their children and feel lonely.

Mothers should be wise and emotionally mature.

Mothers should not be so much attached to their children.

a) Is this reality?

No.

b) What is the reality?

Mothers are what they are. They are attached and dependent.

c) How do I feel when I am attached with these stories?

Sad. Very sad. And lonely. Helpless. Guilty.

d) How do I feel if I detach from this wrong notion?

Yes, these notions are wrong. I cannot help it. Mothers are what

they are. If I detach from my stories, I feel light and peaceful. I can only do my best, but I cannot change mothers.

e) What is preventing me from give up these painful stories?
I have already given them up as this is the most prudent choice for me.

V.   *Whose business?*

a) Am I stepping out of my business and interfering?
Yes. I cannot help it.

b) What is my real business in this moment?
I should not miss myself and feel lonely.
I should not miss my mother and be unhappy.
I should be wise and emotionally mature.
I should be happy and peaceful.
I should love myself.
I should love everybody.
I should love my mother as she is and not expect her to change overnight.
I should help my mother understand the conditionings, but if she does not, it's OK.

VI.   *Why should I give up my real business ever?*
Thank God, I was sad and lonely. Because of that, I feel light and free now. I don't want to feel guilty for no fault of mine. I love my mother. But I accept that mothers can be lonely sometimes.

This is how they will learn and grow.

No reason to give up my real business ever.

Note: Once again, Enat needs to intelligently prioritize. Just living in agitations borne out of thoughtlessness is not good for her. She needs to create an inner peaceful environment first and then decide what she wants to do. She has to clearly and intelligently weigh between going back to Israel and living in France for her studies. Having come to whichever decision, she *should* live by it happily!

Carly

Carly was disturbed that Lisa insulted her. Lisa had a bad relationship with her mother. She got angry with her one day on the phone. When she came back to the room, she started blasting Carly without any rhyme or reason. After that, Carly left her and started living in a different place. But the whole episode made her very angry and sad.

Now she was at the meditation centre, meditating...

I.   *Is it a dream or reality?*

Dream. A bad dream.

a) Is it relevant in this moment?

No. Only living in the moment is relevant.

b) Is it useful in this moment?

No. Nothing is changing. Especially Lisa. And what she has done cannot be undone.

c) Is it conducive to peace in this moment?

No. Not at all.

d) Am I out of it?

No and yes!

II.   *What are the feelings hidden in the dream?*

a) What are the causal feelings?

I like that Lisa should not have insulted me.

I dislike that she insulted me.

I don't like the way our friendship ended.

I would like Lisa to apologize.

b) What are the consequential feelings?

I am angry. The whole episode keeps running in my mind all the time.

I also feel grateful to her sometimes when I remember the good times we had together. That makes me sad afterwards.

c) Do I want to be peaceful?

That is the only thing I want now.

d) Keeping the causal feelings alive, can I attain peace?

No. I need to prioritize. I know that if I expect, I will suffer.

III. *What are the incompleteness equations hidden in the dream?*

I + Lisa should not have insulted me = completeness

I + Lisa's insults = incompleteness

I + Lisa feeling sorry = completeness

I + unapologetic Lisa = incompleteness

a) If these desires gets fulfilled, will you get lasting peace?

No, I don't think so.

b) What is your own history?

I think I somehow attract such a behavior from my friends. More often than not, they start taking me for granted. In this case also, Lisa was angry with her mother. It had nothing to do with me. But she chose to vomit all her anger on me.

Perhaps, I need to learn my lesson finally. Perhaps, I need to be strong and people around me should not get this message that I can be easily walked over.

c) Are you attaching yourself with something permanent?

In a way, no. This incident is over, I understand. If I keep expecting, I will suffer. But my lessons should always remain with me. I also accept that there are more important things in life than getting angry over somebody's behavior.

d) Can incompleteness ever give completeness?

No. I want to drop my X factor for good. Let the world do whatever, I should still be able to remain indifferent and peaceful.

IV. *What are the general conditionings hidden in the dream?*

Friends should respect each other.

Friends should not insult each other.

Friendships should last.

There should not be an abrupt end to a good friendship.

People should not vomit their poison on friends.

a) Is this reality?

No. I wish it were all true. But it is sad that it is not true.

b) What is the reality?

Friends can be callous. Friends can be lethargic.

c) How do I feel when I am attached with these stories?

Angry and sad. Helpless also.

d) How do I feel if I detach from theses wrong notions?

These notions have been very dear to me all my life and I have suffered a lot due to that. Not any more. I need grounding in reality. If I detach, I feel I can understand people better. Why they do what they do – that's more clear to me now. I can accept that people and even friends can be insulting sometimes. They have their X factors which makes them behave so callously. It's OK. I feel compassion for Lisa. I feel silence and kindness in my being.

e) What is preventing me from give up the painful stories?

I am detached and I am free. I don't want to give up my freedom now.

V.   *Whose business?*

a) Am I stepping out of my business and interfering?

Yes. How Lisa behaves is her business. How people behave is their business.

b) What is my real business in this moment?

I should respect myself. My peace of mind is my respect for myself.

I should not insult myself by becoming angry and sad.

I should respect Lisa and understand her.

I should not insult Lisa by getting angry with her even in my mind.

My love for myself should last.

I accept that nothing lasts, not even friendships.

I understand that anything can end abruptly. I should be prepared for everything.

It is OK that some people need to vomit out in order to feel light.

I should not vomit and instead, I should do deep inquiry.

VI. *Why should I give up my real business ever?*

I want to be free. Always. I don't want to give up this state of understanding and compassion anymore.

Questions

I

Q. Why meditation?

A. To become mindful, peaceful, blissful and loveful. To experience the inner joy of freedom. To know the Self.

Q. I am quite conscious of myself. I can do investigation when I am agitated. What is so unique about meditation?

A. Becoming conscious in this manner is the first step. The more important step is to be conscious of the perspective that leads to agitation. Are you aware of your perspectives?

Q. What do you mean by that?

A. Does your happiness come from within you or from outside—from yourself or from people and situations?

Q. It comes from within me, I know. But when I am agitated, I think that it is due to external factors. What does that mean?

A. It means that the understanding is there, but it is not deep enough. It needs to be integrated.

Q. How do you do that?

A. By meditation. Meditation means correcting your wrong perspective and applying the truth to your real life. Please understand that it is not just a routine tool that you may use when you are in distress. It is your life—straightening your priorities; removing the illusions; finding the truth; living in equanimity and inner joy. Does it appeal to you?

Q. Yes. I am slowly understanding.

II

Q. I never knew that it was due to involuntary thoughts that I was not able to meditate. Please tell me what is the right attitude to meditation?

A. It is so beautiful that you have realized that your own mind creates obstacles. They don't come from outside. In order to realize the state of *stable blissful awareness*, all the holes in the mind need to be plugged. The dependence is the biggest hole. You need to be ruthless in the practice as you will see that your mind will play tricks and try to deceive you in many ways.

Keep in mind these four important points:

a) Courage in the wake of all adverse opinions. Others may not understand you; it's OK. You have to understand them and not try to impose your views on them.

b) Indifference to your agitations borne out of false notions. Sincere desire to drop the cherished stories. Let yourself not get duped by your own mind. It is still like a young sapling. You will also need to protect cautiously.

c) Keep the flame of love for yourself alive even if you fail once in a while.

d) Regular and systematic practice. Go on working on yourself until living in your divine nature becomes natural and effortless for you.

Q. I understand the whole process, but it looks like a very difficult task.

A. Take your steps. Just do it. Your desire to climb a big mountain can be fulfilled only by taking steps—one by one. You must start doing the practice diligently and regularly.

III

Q. What do you say of people who are already very loving and considerate to others? Why should they meditate?

A. Are they peaceful also? Do they have equanimity, whatever the situation? Do they experience inner fulfillment or they still live in the illusion that happiness and completeness come from outside?

Compassionate state is only the fourth state on the ladder of evolution. My experience is that it is a lovely state to be in, but it is not the end of the game. It is rather the beginning of spirituality.

Most of the students who get interested in meditation retreats belong to the compassionate state of being. They are wonderful people, but restless. They suffer due to various illusions of understanding. They need to get a good grounding in the right understanding to have a peaceful mind.

Q. If one has a clear direction about dharma, should one meditate even then?

A. You are still concentrating on the externals. You are still believing that happiness comes from outside. This is wrong thinking.

Knowing one's dharma in this sense only means that you understand what ought to be your calling or vocation. That is a necessary step. You will be comparatively happy going to your work place. You will have less disturbing thoughts at least on this account.

Is that the end of life? Are you living just for doing a certain work? Have you realized lasting fulfillment and is your mind peaceful? If yes, you don't need to meditate. If no, you still need to remove the illusions of understanding and realize the inner bliss. How is that possible without meditation?

IV

Q. If one has to go beyond thinking, why do you put so much emphasis on thinking?

A. If you look at the ladder of evolution, you will see that most of the people in the world are still hovering around sensuality and lethargy. That is, their minds are extremely agitated or confused. There are a few who are creative and some are compassionate also.

As you climb the ladder, the mind gets less and less chaotic. But chaos cannot be completely removed without removing the illusions. The happiness-coming-from-outside is the basic misunderstanding. Unless you remove it, there is no possibility that your mind will attain peace as it will keep projecting the related agitations.

How will you remove your involuntary dreaming without removing the illusions of understanding? How can you remove illusions without contemplating deeply on the nature of reality? And this is what meditation is all about.

If you want to remove a thorn from your finger, you need another thorn to take out the first one. Later on, you throw away both of them. When contemplation will become very deep and will get integrated into your veins and arteries, you will be naturally restful and blissful. There will not be much thinking required then. Until then, it is imperative.

Please understand that I am encouraging you to do contemplation right now. It will help in removing the thorns of wrong understanding. It will naturally develop into effortless meditation when you attain maturity. I am not able to agree with those who propound the practice of mindlessness or thoughtlessness in the beginning itself. It is not possible to do that for the beginners. *The higher mind needs to be used to gobble the lower mind*. *Using the right understanding, one removes the wrong understanding*.

V

Q. I am a marathon runner. The state of bliss that you are talking about is attained in long-distance running also. How is it different from meditation?

A. Relief or Cure—what the requirement? It is true that you can attain relief from your mind by running or by doing yogic postures or by some breathing exercises. But your perspective does not change thereby. The wrong beliefs still remain active in the background. In your computer, there are so many programs that run in the background, e.g., the virus-removal programs. You might not be aware that they are active in your computer, but they keep doing their jobs. Similarly, there are programs that keep running in the background of the mind. You don't become aware of them unless you turn your gaze toward them.

If these mental programs are based on wrong notions, they will give you a lot of pain eventually. Even when they are not giving you pain, they do result in excessive restlessness. You cannot remove this state of being just by running a marathon. You will have to bring about corrections in your thinking process.

Moreover, how long can you run? What after that? We have devised countless ways to delay facing ourselves! We watch TV now, we go for a picnic now; our week days are filled with activities and our weekends are also. If we have nothing to do, we get bored and look for avenues so that we may not have to face ourselves. Please understand that nothing external will give lasting happiness. It is impossible!

The question is what do you want—a relief or a cure?

VI

Q. Do you think that in the hectic western world, it is possible to attain lasting peace of mind?

A. It is in this hectic world that I see more opportunity of attaining peace. If you observe closely, you will see many openings. There are so many people here who are now saturated with sensual living. There are communities catering to the growth of compassion. People love helping others in need. Moreover, there is a strongly growing demand for self growth and spirituality. Don't you see how many millions of such books are read by people here? It is a marvelous revolution of understanding that is happening here. I can see that in the next step of evolution, there is going to be more and more desire to realize the inner bliss. If not here, then where?

Q. Don't you think that it is difficult to meditate in such a frenzied living?

A. I am hearing that you are asking the question about yourself. It is no doubt difficult, but who will sort things out for you? Who will do the prioritization for you? Think of the person at a sea shore waiting for all the waves to end so that he can take a plunge in the waters. Is it ever possible? First of all, decide what do you want in your life?

If an angel appears to you now and gives you one boon, what will ask for? Why? Do you want to be in command of your life? Do you want freedom more than anything else? If yes, you will not be asking this question again. You will get going on this path of inner fulfillment and bliss.

VII

Q. What about creativity? Stopping the dreams will affect creativity and intuitions, isn't it?

A. The flow of creativity needs to be differentiated from chaotic agitations of the mind. When the mind is restful, there is not only better concentration on the job at hand, there is also a better possibility for the flow of creative and intuitive thoughts. The more the chaos, the less this possibility.

All great creative works were created by focused minds and not by chaotic and confused minds.

Q. How about planning and learning from your past mistakes? Is that not the same as living in the future or past?

A. Here also, understand the difference between conscious voluntary thinking and unconscious involuntary thoughting. Thinking is very different from running in circles. The former is to be encouraged as it gives you a direction and it helps you grow. The latter is futile in every sense. It just dissipates your energies.

Conscious thinking about past and future is actually

necessary for most of us as it helps in giving the life a positive direction. It helps in keeping one fruitfully busy. Otherwise, there can creep in some lethargy. It has happened with many paratitioners. Be careful.

Q. Does meditation help in bringing about big decisions?

A. The indecisiveness is due to the agitations of the mind. It happens when you are confused about a certain issue. You are not able to weigh the pros and cons clearly. It results in a glut of unmanageable involuntary dreams that hamper the exercise of volition. With meditation, you will bring in strength with the removal of chaos, dilemmas and confusion. You will certainly be able to arrive at clear decisions.

VIII

Q. Going to meditation and facing oneself is scary. I don't want to do that. Is it not better to keep living in darkness?

A. You can of course do that. Nobody can stop you from running away from yourself. But why do you want to do that? I don't think it serves any purpose at all.

What I am hearing from your question is that you don't want to confront the truth that you need to be independent of your sweet crutches—your attachments. You like the illusion that others will make you happy. You dislike any tinkering with your imaginary cocoons.

Pigeons close their eyes when they face cats pouncing on them. They are too scared to face the reality. But closing the eyes will not solve the problem of big cats all around. The biggest ones are living inside you. Where can you run away from them?

Unless the right understanding dawns, the fears cannot be truly overcome. Face your fears. They are just thoughtless stories. If you want happiness in your life—and I am seeing that there is severe dearth of it right now—you will have to confront both your problems and yourself. Running away or shoving things under the carpet is never a solution.

Q. When you talk of controlling the mind, do you mean it as a way of life?

A. Yes. How can you know a certain truth in your meditation and forget it completely when you get up from the seat of meditation?

IX

Q. I am studying for my degree. How do I apply these concepts?

A. When you study, do the thoughts about future haunt you— 'will I get good grades?', 'will I get a good job?' and similar thoughts about your future?

Q. Yes, all the time. But that is natural.

A. Yes, in a way. Don't you think that you have a fixed amount of mental energy and a lot of it gets wasted in futile daydreaming like that? Imagine putting yourself wholeheartedly into the present moment and studying. Will not your concentration be better and therefore your grades also?

Involuntary dreams don't take you anywhere. You just fritter away your energies and become unhappy also. Your efficiency suffers at the same time. Is it a happy state of being?

Q. But the thoughts of the fruits come on their own.

A. That is fine. Don't worry about what you don't create deliberately. You just do your conscious work on removing the wrong notions from your mind. Gradually, this restlessness will fade away on its own.

Secondly, having dreams of fruits does not ensure their materialization in any way. But if you have a restful frame of mind and better concentration, there is a healthy possibility that you will be able to achieve them.

X

Q. How do I know which state of consciousness I am in?

A. Find out your X factors. When you try to meditate, what kind of dreams do you get?

If your dependence is on gossiping, alcohol, drugs, TV etc. and if you do not mind procrastinating, blaming, criticizing and irresponsible living, you may be in the lethargic state of consciousness. If however, you are driven by money, sex and status, you may be in the sensual state. If you get enchanted by creativity, it is creative state. If, on the other hand, you feel for beings and want to help them come out of their suffering, it is the state of compassion. If you like meditating and are working to attain a state of unconditioned happiness and love, you may be in the state of introspection. When you reach the last two states, all objects of dependence are dropped and you are naturally staying in the eternal blissful awareness as this is realized to be your true identity.

Q. But I find myself oscillating between the first five. What should I do?

A. That is beautiful. You have all the potential for freedom, ready to be realized. Try to spend more and more of your conscious time in the states of introspection and compassion. You will need to work for that as the pull of the senses and lethargy are still there. It is like working against gravity. With consistent and systematic practice, you will be able to stay in peaceful awareness effortlessly.

XI

Q. I worry a lot and I think you cannot avoid certain worries like when your child is sick.

A. I think it is not the sickness of the child that gives you worry; it is rather the sickness of *your* child that causes worry. Nature has created the notion of possession and the consequent suffering associated with it. Nature has also created the possibility of understanding that all notions are transitory mental formations. It is very much achievable to live in the state of pure awareness and desireless love at the same time. The question is whether you want to do that...and whether you are ready for that state of pure being.

Q. I think I want to reach there, but it appears to be difficult. I love my child....Can you please tell me the difference between love and attachment?

A. When you love free from expectations, it is love at its best— love just for its own sake. When there are expectations, it is attachment and it causes suffering in the long run. I am not saying that attachment is bad or wrong. I think it is also a wonderful feeling. The love of a mother for her child—wow! I wish I had an iota of that love in my heart. It is amazing for me; it is brilliant. But the only cause of alarm is that most mothers in this world are unhappy. Can we do something about it? I think, yes. Mothers *can,* for sure, learn to love and serve in freedom. It is just a matter of fixing the gaze on this goal and doing deep contemplation to achieve it.

XII

Q. I am a manager in an aviation company in England. I have learnt that if you don't worry, you cannot do your job with passion.

A. What they have taught you is that unless you are whipped, you cannot work—you always need the flogging of desires, goals and achievements to get going. *Actually, it is true!* Yes, for most people in the world, it is true.

However for those, who have set their goal straight for peace and love, it can be counter-productive. You cannot become a worried free man. It is absurd. For you, the requirement is to work with *awareness, happiness and love* in your heart—doing everything with enjoyment, as if it is the last day of your life.

I also think that your productivity increases as you attain balance of mind. When there is less dissipation of mental energies, you will churn out better work. That is, you can become a happy and more efficient worker. Your decision making abilities are also honed when there is enjoyment and freedom in the heart. It does not remain a routine job for you anymore.

I am also not in favor of sacrificing deserving individuals for the sake of organizations. Their (individuals') priorities are different and they need to be encouraged to follow what is best suited for their inner growth. In this way, they will be able to serve the organizations better.

XIII

Q. I met a girl a few days before coming to the retreat. We sat together for sometime in a room. We felt that both of us were gods and were transferring energy to each other. This girl has a boyfriend, but I think that she is now attracted toward me. I am in a dilemma. I am not able to concentrate in meditation. What should I do?

A. Let go.

Some of us have a strange habit of divinizing things in order to justify them. What I can clearly see in this case is the mental monkeys playing their antics. Come back to the basics—she cannot give you lasting fulfillment and you also cannot give her the same. The whole thing might end up in remorse and quarrels.

Secondly, Don't do unto others what you don't want them to do to you. I am sure you don't like getting cheated?

Q. Who likes?

A. Apply the same standards to yourself that you apply to others.

Q. But there are certain things that give satisfaction.

A. The problem of the world is this *'but'*. You know a certain thing to be true, but you don't want to apply it—your desires come in the way.

Your need is to learn how to balance your feelings with right understanding. This world will become a very chaotic place if everybody just follows his desires without considering the effects.

I know that long-term perspective must be taken into account always—if you don't want to suffer later on.

Please understand that what gives you satisfaction today may become a problem tomorrow. Your solutions turn into troubles in due course.

XIV

Q. Without desires and their fulfillment, I don't understand the concept of happiness.

A. You want to say that having desires and then fulfilling them give you a sense of fulfillment.

Q. Yes.

A. Is it *desiring* that gives fulfillment?

Q. The desires keep me going and their fulfillment gives me fulfillment.

A. Which means that you feel unfulfilled without the fulfillment of desires. Suppose you have one hundred years to live. How much time do you think you would give to desiring and working for their fulfillment and how much to the enjoyment of fulfillment?

Q. I think most of my time is spent in working and chasing. I understand what you want to point at.

A. What I am asking is why can't you start from non-desiring? When you *believe* that you must desire in order to get fulfilled and happy, you are unconsciously accepting that your fulfillment will come from objects external. It cannot. It never does *come* from anywhere. You have just created an imaginary void within yourself and now you want to get rid of it. You first make yourself *believe* that there is a void and you are conditioned to fill it up using temporary external means. Even when your desires get fulfilled, you still remain unfulfilled because this illusion of *first unfulfillment and then fulfillment* is still active in you. It will make you chase something else. It goes on until you pass away one day.

XV

Q. Do you want us to become monks?

A. Yes and no. It depends on how you define a monk. If a monk is one who lives by right understanding, yes. If a monk is one who lives in a forest or a monastery, no.
I understand you believe in the illusion that your happiness is dependent upon others. I am only saying that you think about it deeply and if, even after that, your belief is sustained, go on living the way you have been living. Just learn to think. Don't believe in what others make you think.

Q. I may be wrong, but I also feel that I will become like a cabbage if I follow you.

A. Well, how do you define a cabbage?

Q. It does not feel. It cannot love.

A. Do you think a Buddha does not love? I will repeat here that you need to do deep thinking. When you achieve inner fulfillment and freedom, how will you spend your time? You can never become callous. Your whole being will be full of love. You will of course be free from desires and

211

expectations. There will be no heart breaks for you.

I only ask you to question your beliefs. If you do it in the right spirit, you will be free from suffering, that is for sure. It cannot be that you live in harmony with truth and be unhappy also. It cannot be that you live free from illusions and live like a cabbage. You will be a source of love and peace for whosoever comes in contact with you.

When you meditate, you learn to sublimate your feelings. You move from desiring to accepting; from attachment to love; from greed to contentment. You grow toward peace and freedom.

XVI

Q. Are all desires bad?

A. Desires are desires. The consequences are painful. You need to decide what is good and bad *for you*. These are relative terms. If being happy and fulfilled is good for you, desiring will not be helpful.

Q. I just want good concentration. Raising the level of consciousness is not what I want. I want to have desires.

A. That is perfect for you. Please do the 'This Moment. Mindful Moment.' exercise with the breath. It will be helpful.

Q. I also think that you are brainwashing our minds.

A. You are right. I am washing the brains of wrong notions. Is it something bad I am doing, in your view?

Q. Well, we need to think on our own.

A. Precisely. This is what I am also asking you to do. Don't follow anyone else; just your heart. I am only teaching you how to ask your heart and how to find out what is hidden inside you. I am not here to tell you the answers of the deep inquiry. That is what you need to do on your own.

I want that you be objective in your thinking and hence in answering the questions. Drop all your previous stories and then answer the questions from your heart. In my view 'thinking on one's own' means objective thinking and not biased thinking.

Please understand that I only want you to blossom. I have nothing personal to gain from the work. It is for your good that you need to do it.

Further questions and inquiry

Dear Self...readers,

If you have any other questions, you can email them at

zmeditation@gmail.com. Please put 'ZM : Questions' in the subject field.

For doing silent meditation retreats, please inquire at the same email id. Use 'ZM : Retreat Inquiry' as the subject. You can also get information about the retreat at www.zmeditation.com.

8711746R00131

Made in the USA
San Bernardino, CA
19 February 2014